Pervasive Intelligence Now

Pervasive Intelligence Now

Enabling Game-Changing Outcomes in the Age of Exponential Data

Anu Jain

WILEY

Published by John Wiley & Sons, Inc., Hoboken, New Jersey.
Published simultaneously in Canada.

For general information on our other products and services or for technical
support, please contact our Customer Care Department within the United
States at (800) 762-2974, outside the United States at (317) 572-3993 or fax
(317) 572-4002.

Wiley also publishes its books in a variety of electronic formats. Some content
that appears in print may not be available in electronic books. For more
information about Wiley products, visit our web site at www.wiley.com.

Library of Congress Cataloging-in-Publication Data:

Names: Jain, Anu (Business consultant), author.
Title: Pervasive intelligence now : enabling game-changing outcomes in the
    age of exponential data / Anu Jain.
Description: Hoboken, New Jersey : John Wiley & Sons, Inc., [2019] | Includes
    bibliographical references and index. |
Identifiers: LCCN 2018041456 (print) | LCCN 2018042374 (ebook) | ISBN
    978-1-119-55886-6 (Adobe PDF) | ISBN 978-1-119-55885-9 (ePub) | ISBN
    978-1-119-55887-3 (hardcover)
Subjects: LCSH: Business intelligence. | Management—Statistical methods. |
    Organizational change. | Strategic planning.
Classification: LCC HD38.7 (ebook) | LCC HD38.7 .J33 2019 (print) | DDC
    658.4/72—dc23
LC record available at https://lccn.loc.gov/2018041456

Printed in the United States of America

V10004612_091818

Contents

Preface

This isn't so much a book as it is a conversation. Imagine that you and I are seatmates on an airplane, getting ready for a long flight. We introduce ourselves, and I tell you that I work for a large consultancy and help companies with their analytics efforts. You smile and look a bit apprehensive but curious. Then you begin to tell me a bit about yourself. You're in management, or the C-suite, at a large company that has a mature analytics program that could be worse, but could also be better.

As our conversation grows, you mention some of the problems your organization has been having and ask me some general questions. Over the next several hours our talk deepens to cover a broad spectrum of analytics topics and problems that are common to companies as they navigate the often technically and politically fraught process of using analytics to gain insight into their business and enable better decision-making and make those analytics capabilities pervasive in the organization.

This book represents the perspective and advice I'd give you on that airplane. It's not an endorsement of any philosophy, tool set, or technology. Rather, it's a response—born of more than 20 years of experience—to the most common analytics-related issues that I encounter when I speak to people just like you, all over the world.

Also, this book isn't a narrative. You don't have to read it cover to cover (although I hope you will) to get benefit from reading it. It's not linear; each chapter is short and self-contained so you can open this book to any chapter and start reading when it's convenient for you, then put it down and pick it up later if you need to.

You also might not agree with some of my advice, which is great. My hope in writing this book is to start conversations that serve as the springboard to helping you answer some of your most pressing questions and solve a few of your thorniest problems in implementing analytics— to gain a competitive advantage and grow your stakeholder value.

Thanks for reading, and I'd love to hear from you and continue the conversation!

Acknowledgments

I owe a great debt to many people for their contributions to this book. Without their deep industry knowledge and perception, this book would not have been possible. To Simon Moss who contributed outstanding analysis and content on information yield; to Tyler Rebman for his exceptional work on the human side of analytics and cognitive design and for herding all the cats and getting this thing done; to Mike Portell for his terrific contributions on AnalyticOps and driving everyone to do their job and do it well; to Avi Misra for his knowledge of data science and AI; to Bob Montemurro for his insights on DSNs and the cloud; to Jay Irwin for his vast bank of knowledge on data security; to Dave Trier for his leadership in data science and intelligence: They have taught me a great deal about the nature of true enterprise intelligence.

* * *

Simon Moss, Vice President, Industry Consulting and Solutions, Americas. Simon is responsible for consulting, solutions, and services across industrial, healthcare, retail, auto and transportation, financial services, and telecommunications industries. This team will be a leader in the application of high performance business analytics and computing, artificial intelligence and machine learning, intelligent process automation, IoT, and distributed computing solutions. Through these innovations, our objective is clear—to bring creative but real, demonstrable, and rapid business success for our clients.

Dave Trier, Competency Practice Lead, Americas. Dave leads over 350 delivery consultants across the following practices: data science, business intelligence, cognitive design, software engineering, data management, and ecosystem architecture. In his extensive delivery career, Dave has worked with all levels—executives, business leads, technical SMEs, developers—to help companies drive business value from technology and innovation.

Bob Montemurro, Ecosystem Architecture Lead, Americas. Bob brings 20-plus years of experience developing, architecting, and managing enterprise data and business intelligence solutions. With experience in designing and building large-scale enterprise analytic ecosystem solutions across multiple platforms, Bob captures and develops best practices for repeatable professional service delivery across ecosystem architecture and agile data development.

Avi Misra, Americas Data Science Practice Lead, Americas. Avi leads the Data Science practice in Americas that helps businesses realize the promise of artificial intelligence and machine learning. He has 15-plus years of experience in research, development, and deployment of artificial intelligent and machine learning solutions across multiple industries, including advertising and recommendation systems at Amazon, as well as the checkout-free Amazon Go store.

Tyler Rebman, Cognitive Design Practice Lead, Americas. Tyler is responsible for leading the Americas Cognitive Design Practice. As a seasoned services and technology leader with over 20 years of experience, Tyler's team drives the intersection of the left and right brain in analytics. His teams explore, envision, and create the art of the possible and drive end-user adoption of analytical applications that include artificial intelligence, machine learning, and business intelligence.

Jay Irwin, InfoSec Practice Lead, Americas. Jay leads the Enterprise Information Security, Assurance Practice, and Regulatory Compliance Practice for Teradata Center for Enterprise Security. Jay has over 20 years of Information Security and Assurance Management Consulting for Fortune 1000 companies, political subdivisions, and multinational organizations. Jay's specialties include: information security professional services practice management, risk management, information security consulting, information assurance consulting (DoD/federal agencies), cybersecurity consulting and program development, and security architecture assessment and design.

Mike Portell, Chief of Staff, Americas. Mike is Chief of Staff for Teradata Consulting. He is focused on leading strategic initiatives and operation management in a transforming organization. Mike is a 15-year veteran in the consulting and technology space. He was an early employee at Teradata Consulting and led their largest accounts, focused on advanced analytics, open source, and data engineering. Prior to Teradata Consulting, Mike was with Accenture in their R&D unit, focused on deploying emerging technologies.

Introduction

Sophisticated analytics capabilities aren't optional anymore; they're table stakes. What's more, analytics capabilities are changing at a rapid pace. Just in the past decade, the deluge of big data has wrought a vast transformation of the IT landscape. New technologies such as artificial intelligence (AI) and the cloud promise to change the way companies approach analytics and decision-making, as well as data storage and technical infrastructure design.

Additionally, globalization has added pressure to gain efficiencies, connect more intimately with suppliers and customers, and increase top- and bottom-line revenue to maximize shareholder value. To ease these pressures, today's companies must respond more quickly than ever before to customer demands, competition, and market changes. They must understand and drive to meet those outcomes that will have the most impact on their business and enable them to not just survive, but thrive.

However, it's often difficult, with the myriad technologies available, for many companies to get the right analytics infrastructure in place to drive high-impact outcomes. As a result, their business strategies don't often have the intended effect, their competitive edge is blunted, and shareholder value stagnates.

MEETING THE CHALLENGE: MAKING INTELLIGENCE PERVASIVE TO DRIVE HIGH-IMPACT OUTCOMES

So how will companies deal with these pressures and achieve game-changing outcomes? It won't be just by using analytics. Instead of an end in themselves, analytics capabilities are merely a means to an end—a tool to achieve a goal.

1

That goal is to provide information on all facets of the business. But even that's not enough. Leading companies will turn the information gleaned from their analytics activities into true intelligence, and they will embed that data intelligence into their organizational DNA; they will make it pervasive.

How will they do that? Companies that want to realize pervasive data intelligence and drive high-impact outcomes will embrace new technologies; they will get connected; and they will be agile.

They Will Embrace New Technologies

Big data has made traditional business intelligence (BI) and analytics tools almost obsolete—especially for large, complex, or multinational companies. As a result, analytics technologies are undergoing a profound change, in the form of AI. Retailers are already adopting AI technologies for deep learning to manage customer interactions and increase customer satisfaction. Manufacturers have also embraced AI to improve their production, quality, and logistics. In fact, AI-augmented analytics can be applied to nearly every industry and sector.

They Will Get Connected

Instead of linear product and information flows, companies will create digital ecosystems where information flows to and from who and where it's needed, when it's needed, to maximize efficiency throughout the network. Information latency will no longer be an issue, because on-demand, near real-time information flow will create almost instantaneous insights that will be accessible to all interested and authorized parties. Increased information flow speed will provide the insights needed to develop more effective business strategies, which will lead to more business opportunities and help create new strategic advantages.

They Will Be Agile

The foundation of intelligent, connected companies will be an innovative technical infrastructure that supports multiple, dynamic technologies.

That innovative infrastructure is the cloud. But not just any cloud. Companies that thrive going forward will gain flexibility by combining their analytics and cloud technologies into an intelligent cloud, so that their analytics aren't simply supported by the cloud—they're integrated with it. Intelligent clouds will enable companies to deploy the latest and most sophisticated analytics capabilities, combined with flexible, secure, cloud storage—and to spin up or down as needed, based on project demands and technology requirements.

WHAT'S AHEAD

In this book, we look at some strategies to help companies make intelligence pervasive. We discuss how companies can define and measure high-impact outcomes and use analytics technology effectively to achieve them. We also look at the technology needed to implement the analytics necessary to achieve high-impact outcomes—both from an analytics tool and technical infrastructure perspective.

Additionally, we also touch on ancillary, but critical, topics such as data security and governance. Traditionally, these topics may not be a part of analytics discussions but they are essential in helping companies maintain a secure environment for their analytics and access the quality data needed to gain critical insights and drive better decision-making.

And, really, that's what this book is about: helping you understand how you can develop strategies and leverage technology to make data intelligence pervasive and drive those outcomes that have the biggest impact on your business. So, let's get started.

PART **I**

Strategies to Make Intelligence Pervasive

New technologies and automation have increased fraud and compliance risk, at a time when customers are demanding innovative new products and services, and shareholders are demanding that companies unlock the greatest value from all their physical, intellectual, and digital assets. There's no break—no time to breathe before the next problem hits.

These challenges are exacerbated by fragmented intelligence. Analytics capabilities are siloed, so decision-making is hobbled by poor insight into customer behavior and operations. Innovation is stifled and customer satisfaction plummets. Losses from compliance violations and fraud mount, and supply chains become sluggish. This lethal mix leaves many companies foundering and unable to satisfy anyone: shareholders, customers, or regulatory agencies. The need to have sound strategies that enable you to make data intelligence pervasive and compete with your analytics capabilities is paramount.

The strategies you develop to make intelligence pervasive must be finely attuned to achieving high-impact outcomes—those outcomes that power your success. What's more, it's essential to understand the value you get from data—the information yield—so that you can make decisions on whether to add to, or change, your analytics capabilities and/or technical infrastructure.

As for your technical infrastructure, the strategies you use to store data and access it for analytics capabilities will play an outsized role in helping—or hindering—your effort to drive high-impact outcomes. The cloud has emerged as a go-to option for many companies, but there are a multitude of cloud-deployment options and you must have a clearly developed cloud strategy, with a trusted vendor partner to wring value from the cloud.

In addition to realizing the transformative power of the cloud for managing data workloads gaining flexibility, companies that succeed will leverage digital connectivity to revolutionize the way they acquire resources, move products, and serve customers.

Successful companies will also realize that analytics systems should be built with the people who will use them in mind. They won't buy technology just because it's "hot." Instead, they will use the principle of cognitive design to build applications that meet users' needs and facilitate better insight and decision-making.

These companies will also understand that, even though data governance and security aren't necessarily the most exciting topics, they are critical to the success of their analytics effort. If users don't trust the answers they get from the system, they won't use it, and if customers and partners don't trust you to shepherd their data, they'll defect in droves.

In short, companies that succeed in the pressure-cooker of intense global competition and ever-increasing demands to build shareholder value will devise successful strategies to help them embed intelligence at the cellular level to define and achieve business outcomes that have the biggest positive impact on their future.

CHAPTER **1**

Achieving High-Impact Outcomes—An Overview

The sole reason to embed data intelligence into your organization—to make it pervasive—is to help you make better decisions that lead to achieving high-impact outcomes. To get the information you need to make better decisions, it's crucial to have the ability to develop customized analytics applications quickly, and scale them up or down based on intelligence needs.

This means that you are becoming—or need to become—like a software company, whether you want to or not. Therefore, your IT strategy and technology expectations must reflect this premise.

For example, artificial intelligence and digital supply networks can enable you to become more agile by providing the ability to better understand and interpret your environment and become more responsive to business and market needs. However, the foundation of this agility is the technical infrastructure that supports all these dynamic technologies. If that infrastructure is not cutting-edge and flexible, it can't support innovative technologies.

Software companies (meaning your company!) need technical infrastructures that are more akin to those of utility companies. On a hot summer day, do you contact your local electric supplier to make more wattage available to your house in order to run your air conditioner? No, you get billed for what you utilize.

The same is true for intelligence capabilities. Establishing the infrastructure enables you to quickly access the resources you need to develop and deploy intelligence capabilities when and where you need them, and to make that intelligence pervasive.

Pervasive data intelligence is all about driving game-changing outcomes. It doesn't matter what problems you have, or which tools you buy to solve them, it's the results that matter. How well did your strategy work? How well did it solve your problems and enhance your ability to compete in a cutthroat environment that kills businesses without mercy? How well did it enable you to meet your high-impact outcomes?

To create those high-impact outcomes—outcomes that have a significant effect on your company's bottom line and that will help you thrive in today's digitally transformed marketplace—you need three things:

1. The right data to help you gain the insights you seek
2. A technical architecture and environment that stresses flexibility and scalability
3. Operational excellence, facilitated by the right data and the right technology, integrated with your organizational operations

Simple, right? No: but it is doable.

Figure 1.1

THE RIGHT DATA

Customer demands to innovate and provide better, more personalized, customer service—coupled with shareholder demands to increase share value and speed their ROI—have created a critical need for companies to better leverage data for decision-making. However, amidst the inundation of big data, it's often difficult to tease out valuable data from noise.

To get the data you need, you first have to understand your business needs. By asking the right questions, you can get the answers you seek, and get started on wringing the data you need out of the wash of data that floods your company every day.

First, ask your managers and knowledge workers what data they need to do their jobs. That's the data that will drive value and create those high-impact outcomes that will help you thrive. Next, look at the questions you're asking. What data do you need to answer those questions and gain those critical insights that speed and enhance decision-making?

> It's not enough anymore to satisfy your customers. You must delight them. Customers want to feel as if you know them—what they need, what they want, and, most importantly, what they don't know they want.

Once you've gotten a handle on the data your people need to do their jobs and to answer the questions you have, put that data to use. Ask how you can use the data to improve your customer service. It's not enough anymore to satisfy your customers. You must delight them.

To delight them, it's critical to create a sense of greater intimacy between your business and your customers. Customers want to feel as if you know them—what they need, what they want, and, most importantly, what they don't know they want.

Next, use that data to innovate—both in terms of what you offer the market and how you operate your business. Social media has changed the market landscape and businesses that don't constantly innovate die more quickly than ever. Innovation won't be possible, however, unless your business is operating at its optimal level. To do that, you must constantly innovate your operations to achieve and maintain operational excellence.

Finally, the right data can also help you mitigate risk. There's no reward without risk, but too much risk leads to disaster. What's more, the types of risks have multiplied exponentially (fraud, cybersecurity, market, economic, political) and it's essential to evaluate them appropriately and manage them effectively. It's essential to integrate technology—especially AI—into all aspects of risk management.

There's one caveat to getting and using the right data. Do it quickly, so that you can move on to the next step: designing the architecture and environment you need to leverage that data.

THE RIGHT TECHNICAL ARCHITECTURE AND ENVIRONMENT

Creating customer intimacy requires massive amounts of data and complex, sophisticated analytics capabilities—think AI and machine learning. Risk management also requires complex analytics and sophisticated analytics, but it requires ironclad security as well. Continual innovation and operational excellence require it all—big data, sophisticated analytics, and security—but it also require flexibility in your IT infrastructure. You must be able to spin up or spin down, according to your information or project needs.

> The key to determining what technology options will work best is to look at those options through the prism of your business outcomes.

The key to determining what technology options will work best for your business is to look at those options through the prism of your business outcomes. It's imperative to be honest with yourself about where you're starting from, and where you can realistically go, over multiple time horizons.

Construct an infrastructure and analytics maturity model. Be realistic about how much you can accomplish, but work fast. It's critical to start fast and prove value, both from a competitive standpoint and to satisfy C-suite demands and access the money you need to build your optimal state.

Any technology-architecture design you choose to help you achieve your outcomes should have three key capabilities: it should have the ability to accommodate multistructured data; it should be flexible enough to incorporate new technologies as they arise, and as your needs change; and it should be scalable to grow as you do.

To gain these capabilities, more and more organizations are taking advantage of digitization and leveraging the transformative value of the cloud. By moving your analytics applications and technical infrastructure to the cloud, you can gain a flexible, scalable platform that helps you implement your desired technical architecture—now and in the future—and achieve cost-effectiveness and certainty.

When you don't have to wrangle with applications and infrastructure management, you free up resources to focus on proving the business value of your efforts by achieving those high-impact outcomes that drive success.

There are many cloud options: public, private, and hybrid clouds; intelligent clouds that mingle the cloud with analytics technology (my personal favorite); and machine-learning algorithms to augment those analytics. The list is almost endless. However, the cloud options you choose must be purchased with the goal of enabling you to meet those high-impact business outcomes that you've defined. If you don't have clear outcomes in mind, and match the technology to those outcomes, the technology is useless.

OPERATIONAL EXCELLENCE

Once you have the data you need, and the right technical architecture and environment, the next step is to leverage those assets to improve your operations. Analytics, when embedded in a flexible, cloud-based architecture and infused into your business operations, can help you drive operational excellence.

The reason most executives give for implementing new analytics initiatives—any technology initiative, really—is to enable them to improve the way they do business and satisfy their customers. But operational excellence is more than that.

> The cloud options you choose must be purchased with the goal of enabling you to meet those high-impact business outcomes that you've defined. If you don't have clear outcomes in mind, and match the technology to those outcomes, the technology is useless.

First, it's a commitment to innovation. We touched on innovation earlier—both in terms of products and operations. Analytics and innovation have a symbiotic relationship, a virtuous circle. The answers you gain from your analytics can drive innovation, to be sure, but innovation can also spur new analytics implementations as the business grows and new products become necessary to meet growing market demands.

Operational excellence also requires clear strategic direction and focus, as well as leadership, to drive results. This is where embedding intelligence—making it pervasive throughout the organization—pays off. The insights you gain can help you develop more successful strategies and hone your focus on defining those outcomes that will have the biggest impact on the bottom line and drive shareholder value. Leadership that is committed to leveraging technology and managing by insight, rather than gut instinct, can drive strategy implementation and achievement of those high-impact outcomes. Long-term operational excellence is a matter of redefining those high-impact outcomes as customer needs and market conditions change.

DRIVING HIGH-IMPACT OUTCOMES WITH PERVASIVE INTELLIGENCE

The relationship between high-impact outcomes and pervasive data intelligence is clear. Insight is key. The right data, the right technical infrastructure, and striving for operational excellence will help you implement the analytics solutions you need to get critical intelligence and insights about your business environment. If you embed that intelligence into your organization—if you make it pervasive—you will gain an enterprise perspective on your organizational information, and you can use that perspective to drive those high-impact outcomes.

CHAPTER 2

New Metrics for Intelligence— Information Yield

Pervasive intelligence pays off, in the form of better insight gleaned from the information resident in your organizational systems. But how do you measure the effectiveness—the yield—of your information, especially across tools and technologies? How do you know if you're getting the most out of your organizational intelligence?

Over the past 25 years, business intelligence (BI) and analytics technologies have revolutionized business decision-making. Tableau, TiBCO, Qlik, Cognos, and SAS, to name just a few, have all made tremendous strides. Open source has democratized BI applications and models and opened up huge innovation opportunities.

There have also been major advances in visualization techniques, as well as amazing growth in analytic consumables. And then there are the breakthroughs in AI and machine learning, both of which offer incredible promise in establishing situational fidelity and decision lineage in huge, complex enterprises. So why do so many companies struggle to wring value from their analytics programs? Why is it common that 80% of analytics costs consist of building the environment to create value, yet the environment creates no value at all?

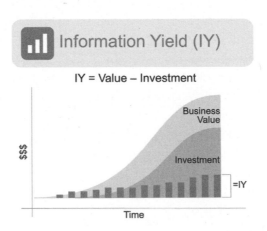

Figure 2.1

INFORMATION YIELD—THE JOURNEY FROM 2D TO 3D IN ANALYTICS

The problem lies in the fact that the momentum of innovation typically focuses on the easy part of solving business problems. It almost always assumes that everything is on one plate, ready and clear, so that all you need to do is analyze, investigate, mine, discover, and conclude. It's an assumption that has led to countless project failures and forms the basis for just as many failed business opportunities. Why?

To use a transport analogy, prior to 2000, BI was one-dimensional—like a train—only able to go backwards and forwards between data source and destination. Second and third generation analytics and BI added another dimension, able to calibrate different sources and establish more complex models.

> Simply put, the analytical breakthroughs we are experiencing are being deployed in an antiquated two-dimensional integration and implementation model that has not changed for 30 years.

You can look at these technologies as akin to a train, now able to travel two-dimensionally because they've been taken off restrictive one-dimensional tracks, and they've added the dimension of lateral movement.

Yet both of these transport types require predefined "paths," a track or road that someone else designed, built. Simply put, the analytical breakthroughs of today are being deployed in an antiquated two-dimensional integration and implementation model that has not changed for 30 years.

They satisfy the needs of travelers to get around efficiently, but that's as far as they go. The drawback is that this type of analytics deployment forces analysis to wait for the data to be ready: prepared and laid out ahead of the analytical tool so it can be used effectively. It works, but you sense there could be more "there" there.

Therein lies the problem. This two-dimensional approach requires huge amounts of data preparation, and a big, costly IT footprint for the technology to operate effectively. Yet the data and other elements to make analytics and BI effective are increasingly distributed, on the edge, part of the "Internet of Things."

What's more, they're exponentially increasing in complexity, size, distribution, and heterogeneity. With current deployment approaches, you're typically stuck with figuratively building more roads or tracks to make your analytics work effectively as data and value sources grow.

This is a not a volume or big data issue. Rather it's a problem of increasing data distribution, diversity, and access. However, the data distribution issue continually undermines the value of more complex, valuable reporting and analytical breakthroughs—ones that require a massive amount of calibration to produce a competitive edge and risk transparency. This is where technologies like edge computing, microservices, and the API world are beginning to offer interesting solutions to a significant category of problems, especially as self-service demands grow.

The Third Dimension

To meet distribution challenges, a third dimension is needed—akin to an aircraft with the ability to fly and travel to wherever data and the value sources are located. Backwards, forwards, left, and right are now augmented by up and down.

Complete, unfettered navigation of data around the enterprise provides the degree of flexibility needed to improve efficiency in the journey to your destination.

> The data distribution issue continually undermines the value of more complex, valuable reporting and analytical breakthroughs—ones that require a massive amount of calibration to produce competitive edge and risk transparency.

THREE FOUNDATIONAL STEPS TO DRIVE TRANSFORMATION

Gaining such flexibility is a gigantic problem—one that faces companies in every industry. You'll hear people say that the problem is unsolvable, that it will always undercut analytic effectiveness.

They're wrong. To be sure, it's not easy but it can be solved. Companies that solve it will be the ones that dominate their future markets and grow their bottom line. Because how you define, quantify, and manage your information assets as part of your core strategy will determine your competitive landscape and advantage.

There are three steps that will enable you to create value, speed digital transformation, and yield competitive advantage:

1. **Culture and organization.** This is the hardest part. It's critical to align your organization, and the resulting data architecture must to be integrated as well. Information siloes must be removed and data must to be structured horizontally, by purpose. This "process-relevant" data alignment drives out opacity, and it provides a navigable environment. What's more, it reduces data management OpEx (operating expense) by an order of magnitude. Achieving this horizontal "fit for purpose" organizational structure is critical to drive up the yield of information from data. It also solves a huge cost and margin issue that will be the existential challenge for survival for many large enterprises in the future.

2. **Data foundation.** You can't break the laws of physics when it comes to data. Whether you standardize data at the write level (relational), at the read level (Hadoop), or even at the edge, you still have to homogenize data to extract value and increase information yield. Trying to work around data standardization simply adds inefficiency and expense to the process and will continue to do so.

3. **Analytics democratization.** If data is the new oil, we should stop building oil rigs and focus on building refineries to start to extract value. Analytics democratization is driving huge innovations, and the speed of innovation is remarkable. For example, TensorFlow is now the second most popular analytics engine after SQL, yet Google released it to the market less than three years ago. Philosophical arguments between different languages, engines, and tools are now pointless. Instead, analytics efficiency requires environments that support them all, as well as the new ones being invented, against common processes and data. The cloud and as-a-service models offer a compelling future that will free up analytical creativity, push up quality, and scale and drive down architecture management costs.

No matter what, business solutions should not be projects where 80% of the cost is spent creating the environment to create value, but creates no value at all. Rather they should be low-cost, high-impact, rapid-to-develop analytical lens viewing the same operating data not matter what problem they target.

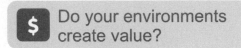

Do your environments create value?

80 cents on every project dollar is spent before a single penny of transparency or value can be created.

Nearly 60 cents of that spend is an exact repeat of every project that has come before it.

Figure 2.2

Address these foundational steps and you can encourage creativity and drive exponential transformation. Consistency and discipline can finally be reconciled with creativity and innovation. Moreover, you can focus diversification and costs together to drive competitiveness and margin. This is information yield.

BIG DATA AND ITS IMPACT ON INFORMATION YIELD

Big data is here to stay, and it's only getting bigger. No doubt it will continue to generate value, but from an ROI perspective. If companies don't update their deployment and data access models, it won't be much help besides creating some impressive sales for service and technology providers.

There are some impressive new technologies that are designed to solve the balance of data velocity, agility, and quality. However, if you want to increase your margins and competitiveness while holding technology costs in line, you must begin to look at different ways to access data, derive quality, and create value.

Decentralize and Orchestrate

To create more value from data, it's essential to decentralize storage and access to it. Build a model where data access, analysis, and quality management are fully distributed and orchestrated across a network, so that you're taking analysis to the data source rather than trying to cobble all the sources into a single construct before material analysis.

> So how do we solve this quadratic equation of balancing velocity, agility, and quality without breaking the bank? Decentralize and orchestrate.

By moving analysis from the front to the back of the value process, you can cut your TCO (total cost of ownership) in half. Analysis speed is enhanced, since intelligence is derived at the data source. You also become more agile, since a network is infinitely more flexible than a complex, stacked data structure. Finally, you can be assured of higher-quality information, because you've moved the solution to the business problem closer to the data source that helps you solve it, without going through an intermediary or using a drawn-out normalization process.

Rather ironically, if you're serious about increasing your data quality and analysis speed, it's essential to shift back to a more distributed strategy. The process has come full circle: from mainframes to PCs, then shifting back to centralized computing/applications/web services. Now increasing organizational complexity demands a return to distributed processing, access, and required data quality.

Have a Plan

Highly complex enterprise environments will not be optimized by one element alone. Instead you'll need to develop multiple strategies and wrap them into a cohesive plan:

1. Centralize big data for behavior detection and insight generation.
2. Fine-tune transactional applications which execute tactical business activities and composite solutions.
3. Integrate and orchestrate disparate points of value from across the enterprise, and do it with a distributed, resilient, and scalable methodology.

The key is to solve all three elements with a well-orchestrated plan, based on early and constantly measurable success, avoiding the ridiculous expenditures and project risks of the past—and fully exploiting some impressive breakthroughs in data management and noninvasive transformation that are currently hitting the market.

INFORMATION YIELD AND PERVASIVE INTELLIGENCE

Information yield is simply a measuring stick for the effectiveness of your efforts at embedding intelligence into your organizational processes and operations. There are no specific guidelines or measuring units. The proof is in your decision-making and intelligence capabilities. Do you have the information you need to make the decisions that enable you to meet the goals you set and compete effectively, to realize those outcomes that have the most impact on your business? If you can answer "yes" to that question most of the time, you're on your way to pervasive data intelligence.

CHAPTER 3

The Cloud— The Foundation for Pervasive Intelligence

mbracing new technologies is a foundational component of embedding data intelligence in your organization—of making it pervasive. Making intelligence pervasive gives you the ability to better understand and interpret your environment and become more responsive to business and market needs. The foundation of this pervasive intelligence is a cutting-edge technical infrastructure that supports dynamic technologies. That cutting-edge infrastructure is the cloud.

CLOUDS—WHAT'S BEST FOR YOU?

There are many types of cloud: on-premises, public, private, hybrid—with ever-changing variations on each of those terms, according to the particular cloud service provider. How can you know what's best for you? It's simple. What's right for you is the configuration that lets you worry the least, while achieving the best business outcomes.

- On-premises clouds
    On-premises clouds offer the ultimate in security and control, but you have to provide the footprint, the physical hardware, security, and IT resources to manage the entire infrastructure. With public clouds, you don't have to provide the hardware, but you still have to provide resources to manage the process, and there's the issue of sharing space and of possible outages.

CLOUD OPTIONS

- On premises—The ultimate in security and control, but space and sharing may be issues down the line.
- Private—Dedicated to you, but hosted by a provider. Takes time to ramp up or ramp down.
- Managed—Fully managed by a provider; lets any company take advantage of the cloud regardless of resources.
- Hybrid—The best of all worlds: ultimate flexibility in a borderless environment where you can ramp up or down as needed.

- Private clouds
    Private clouds are dedicated to you, but they're hosted on a cloud provider's infrastructure. However, you still have to

have a cadre of resources to interact with the cloud provider and manage the process overall. Private clouds are secure, to be sure, but they're also limiting in that you need time and planning to ramp up or down.

- Managed clouds

  Managed cloud models are those in which a cloud service provider fully manages your cloud environment and analytics infrastructure. The cloud utilized can either be public or private, or a combination thereof. Managed clouds are great for those companies that don't have the resources to implement or manage the large data sets and the concomitant infrastructure it takes to perform deep, complex analytics.

- Hybrid clouds

  Hybrid clouds offer the ultimate combination of all the types discussed here. With a hybrid model, you can combine managed or self-controlled, on-premises, private, and public cloud deployments in any combination, depending on your needs. You can orchestrate them to work together to meet on-demand data and analytics requirements, creating a borderless environment that enables you to focus on your analytics without having to worry about where the data you're accessing resides. You can ramp up or down at will, with minimal or no disruptions. The resources needed on your part are minimal, but more than with managed clouds.

The bottom line is this: the right choice for you is the one that will best achieve your desired business outcomes, and that's within your human and monetary resource budget. That's all that matters.

CHOOSING THE RIGHT VENDOR PARTNER TO HELP YOU FULFILL THE PROMISE OF THE CLOUD

Once you've made the decision to invest in the cloud, aside from choosing the right hosting and deployment model, there are several concerns that you'll still need to address to achieve an optimal implementation—one that can grow with you and continue to meet your needs as they change.

There are five areas of concern to discuss with any potential cloud-services vendor to ensure that you're getting the right cloud services for your organization. If you choose the right vendor partner, you can realize the enormous transformative value of the cloud and embrace the digital revolution, accelerating your outcomes and increasing topline revenue.

1. Seamless data workload migration and account management

As an inviolable rule, migrating data workloads to the cloud should cause only minimal—or preferably no—business disruptions. It's critical to choose a vendor partner with a tool set that enables automated and seamless migration to minimize downtime. Utilization monitoring should also be straightforward, preferably via a single console that automates as many management and monitoring functions as possible.

> Your cloud deployment options should be flexible, and the vendor you choose should give you the option to deploy in a single environment or over a combination of hybrid environments.

2. Flexible deployment options

Whether it's your vendor's private cloud—such as Teradata's Intellicloud™—or public clouds such as Amazon Web Services™ (AWS), Microsoft Azure™, or any other cloud services provider, your deployment options should be flexible, and the vendor you choose should give you the option to deploy in a single environment or over a combination of hybrid environments, in case you don't want to move all your data to the cloud. One caveat, though. Mission-critical systems, such as data warehouses, should be deployed in a single environment to ensure consistency of data access.

3. Data and systems availability

If your information systems go down, you're dead in the water. Historically, one argument for not moving enterprise workloads to the cloud has been data and application availability concerns. However, there are vendors out there that will guarantee near 100% availability in their SLA (service level agreement). Speed is an issue too. Access speeds should be as if the data is on-premises—or faster. Things happen, and nothing is 100% perfect. But if you choose the right vendor, they'll spell out their availability speed and guarantee it, so data and application availability won't be a concern.

4. Flexibility and scalability

Business, and thus data, needs change—both as you grow and as the market changes. It's a fact of life. Your cloud vendor's suite of offerings should be built around helping you embrace change and growth. Some cloud providers only offer storage and management, which is fine if you already have a robust analytics structure. However, there are vendors that provide both flexible data storage and analytics and database software as a service, which effectively offers you a smorgasbord of options to scale up or change configurations and applications as your needs change, without having to invest in new analytics applications when yours no longer fit your needs.

5. Security

Perhaps the greatest concern for CIOs looking to move their data to the cloud is security. It should be your vendor partner's number one concern as well. Make sure that your vendor's security infrastructure covers the entire spectrum of security needs, including physical security, network security, data protection, monitoring, and access controls. Their security protocols must support secure connections for data transmission. Data should be encrypted, both during transfer and at rest, through self-encrypting drives on a dedicated infrastructure.

THE CLOUD—NOT OPTIONAL FOR PERVASIVE INTELLIGENCE

The cloud isn't really optional anymore. It's becoming a fundamental piece of most companies' technical infrastructure. The flexibility and scalability the cloud provides can enable you to make intelligence pervasive and more agile and responsive to your business and market needs. Implementing some form of cloud technology is really no longer a question. The questions that do remain are which cloud option(s) will work best for your information and security needs, and how to choose the right vendor partner to give you the availability, security, and flexibility you need to grow your bottom line. Answer those, and you'll be well on your way to becoming a more agile, successful enterprise.

CHAPTER **4**

Perpetual Connectivity— Digital Supply Networks

We've focused extensively so far on making data intelligence pervasive to achieve those high-impact outcomes that can help you succeed and increase shareholder value. One critical component of any organization's effort to improve their business outcomes is how well they manage their supply chain. However, the traditional data supply chain is dying. It's being replaced by perpetually connected, digital supply networks (DSN).

A DSN is an ecosystem where information flows to and from who and where it's needed, when it's needed, to maximize efficiency throughout the network. Information latency is no longer an issue, because on-demand, near real-time information flow creates almost instantaneous insights that are accessible to all interested and authorized parties.

On a macro level, increased information flow speed provides the insights needed to develop more effective business strategies, which leads to more business opportunities and helps create new strategic advantages.

> Increased information flow speed provides the insights needed to develop more effective business strategies, which leads to more business opportunities and helps create new strategic advantages.

DSNs DEFINED

When you create a DSN, you do truly leave the old supply chain mentality behind. Information no longer flows linearly. Instead, you create an ecosystem where information flows to and from who and where it's needed, when its needed, so that efficiency is maximized throughout the network. Information latency is no longer an issue, because on-demand, near real-time information flow creates almost instantaneous insights that are accessible to all interested and authorized parties.

DSNs—WHAT THEY CAN DO FOR YOU

The benefits of these freed-up, on-demand information flows are enormous. First, more timely information can help you reduce costs by improving efficiency. The back-and-forth data flows can also help you gain the information you need to make product improvements more quickly, which results in more satisfied customers. More satisfied customers leads to a better reputation, and with that reputation and better information in the hands of your management and salespeople, your sales effectiveness can soar.

On a macro level, increased information flow speed gives you the insights you need to develop more effective business strategies, which leads to more business opportunities and helps you create new strategic advantages.

It's all about the flow—and the speed. If you know more things more quickly than your competitors, you can make quicker decisions and meet market demands faster, which makes you flexible enough to change with the markets—and you know they don't ever sit still.

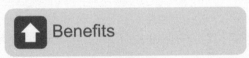

Benefits

- Deeper Insights
- Better Decisions
- Improved Products
- Improved Efficiency
- More Sales Effectiveness
- Increased Customer Satisfaction
- Strategic Advantage
- Improved Bottom Line

Challenges

- Talent Gap—Skills Squeeze
- Dirty Data
- Siloed Data and Systems
- Lack of Connectivity
- "Yeah, buts"
- Political Issues

Figure 4.1

DSN CHALLENGES

As with anything worth having though, there are some challenges to building a true DSN: They're daunting, but not insurmountable, and it'll be worth it in the end to meet them.

Talent will be your first obstacle. Advanced analytics capabilities are at the heart of any DSN. And, if you haven't been hiding under a rock for the past five years, you know that the demand for analytics skills is currently outpacing supply. Fortunately, that's changing. More universities are turning out more quant jocks these days, and more IT people are re-skilling to meet the need.

Data management will be your next hurdle. If you don't have clean, organized data, it will be hard to make it flow smoothly through the ecosystem. Governance is key, along with programs to remove information silos across your enterprise and then from your supply network at large, and building a consistent, high-quality data set for your supply network—end to end.

Unfortunately, perhaps the biggest challenge you'll have to overcome is the "yeah-buts." Yeah, but we're doing fine with what we have—why should we invest millions in some supply matrix technology we don't understand? Yeah, but can you show the business value before we spend all that money? Yeah, but do we have the buy-in from our stakeholders and partners that we need to pull this thing off? The list is endless, but you get my point.

> Political challenges may represent the biggest threat to your DSN project. Do everything you can to educate all stakeholders—your board, your C-suite colleagues, your suppliers, and your customers.

These political challenges may represent the biggest threat to your DSN project. Do everything you can to educate all stakeholders—your board, your C-suite colleagues, your suppliers, and your customers. Build a sound business case to show them how building a DSN will benefit them. There's a litany of information out there about the benefits and value of it. As the caveman commercials say, "do a little research." Don't just build it. They will not come. Build the business case. Show the value. Get the buy-in.

THE BENEFITS OF A DSN ILLUSTRATED

Companies that create DSNs are faster, smarter, and more flexible than ever—and they and their end customers both reap the benefits.

As an example, let's take the case of a consumer products manufacturer that was facing serious, existential challenges with quality and costs. This manufacturer was under increased regulatory scrutiny because they'd had to issue several safety recalls over a five-year span. Their products tended to either not function correctly or, in some cases, to spontaneously ignite. Not a good look.

Because of lack of supply chain integration, they were forced into a reactive mode to solve problems. It took them too long to identify issues and to fix the problems, and they couldn't track how effective their fixes were in the long term. Their warranty expenses were astronomical, and their reputation was sinking fast.

Their solution was to create a DSN. They built a technical infrastructure than enabled them to use cutting-edge technologies like embedded sensors on parts to capture real-time performance data. They also integrated data from all their suppliers to form a complete picture of their parts' chain of custody. This data was coupled with textual quality and safety event data and stored in a data lake to facilitate quick retrieval and integration.

Next, they used advanced analytics tools such as probability analysis and clustering to explore their data. They used a simplified GUI (graphical user interface) and dashboards to enable users to see the data they needed, when they needed it—to quickly deliver actionable insights.

The result? To be sure, they were able to catch production problems more quickly, but the real bonus was that they were able to integrate their supply network and leverage big data and advanced analytics to improve quality and prevent those problems in the first place. They had insight into every facet of their production process to ensure that every step in that process was tracked, monitored, and tweaked to deliver peak performance.

Everyone, from suppliers to logistics partners, to each production facility, had access to the same data set and could identify issues before they became explosive problems. The company's warranty expense decreased over time as quality increased, the government regulators eased off, and their reputation was salvaged—creating an environment where they could increase top line revenue and long-term growth.

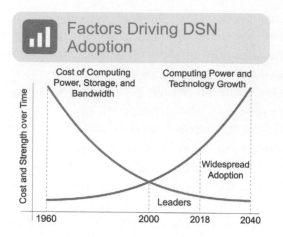

Figure 4.2

DSNs AND THE REALIZATION OF PERVASIVE INTELLIGENCE

It won't be a simple task to embrace digital transformation and build a comprehensive DSN, but that DSN will be a critical component to achieving pervasive data intelligence. Indeed, the connectivity and end-to-end information provided by a DSN is the epitome of pervasive intelligence. It won't be easy, though. The effort will be rife with challenges, and it will consume a large chunk of your resources in the near future.

You really don't have an option, however. Traditional supply chain processes and logistics-management theory simply won't cut it in this hyper-competitive, always-on, global environment. Even the smallest companies are affected by globalization, and customers are increasingly demanding faster innovation and shorter product-delivery cycles. To meet your challenges and thrive, it's a fundamental imperative to begin building your DSN.

CHAPTER 5

Intelligence Analytics and Cognitive Design—The Human Factor in Pervasive Intelligence

Making data intelligence pervasive isn't just about analytics and implementing the latest and greatest technology. In fact, if you focus exclusively on technology and expect it to be a savior, your efforts to embed intelligence throughout the organization won't provide you with the answers you seek. Instead, let your business needs lead the way when you're developing any analytics program. Fundamentally, any analytics initiative is deployed to solve business issues. If you don't understand those issues—and the needs of the people who are knee-deep, trying to address them—your efforts to make intelligence pervasive will miss the mark.

Truly pervasive intelligence that pairs technology with its human users to ensure that the technology follows the human lead will drive your analytics success. This intelligence is powered by design thinking and human-centered design methods—by intelligent analytics.

Design thinking and human-centered design methods can help reveal the unique needs and insights that, when solved, provide both financial value-driven by end-user stickiness. An intelligent, connected, and agile organization can research and solve problems creatively using a diverse team, and rapidly iterate to provide end-to-end solutions that meet end-user needs. Instead of technology, business engagement drives the long-term adoption of analytical ecosystems and produces higher information yield.

It all starts with empathy. With a design methodology that presupposes empathy as its foundation, intelligent analytics can revolutionize how companies achieve high-impact outcomes—from creating customer intimacy to AI-driven operations.

Intelligent analytics can help you become more perceptive, decisive, and responsive to challenges. It can help you understand not only what's happening, but also why it's happening—and most critically—what might happen in the future so that you can begin to control that future and make it work for you, not against you.

> With a design methodology that presupposes empathy as its foundation, intelligent analytics can revolutionize how companies achieve high-impact outcomes.

If you leverage human-centered, cognitive design approaches to facilitate the definition of business outcomes, the engagement of end users, the clarity for all teams responsible for delivery, and the stakeholder and sponsorship you need for success, you can achieve those high-impact outcomes that are so critical to your top- and bottom-line growth.

However, there's a caveat: Intelligent analytics capabilities must be deployed in weeks, not months. The analytics deployed must combine the promise of data science with rich insights to generate models that can quickly move from proof-of-concept to measurable ROI (return on investment).

WHY COGNITIVE DESIGN?

Cognitive design is all about solving specific problems for real people, while being empathetic to how they think, feel, and act. The simple, yet powerful, premise is that empathy will allow you to understand problems in a new light and therefore see new opportunities to solve them. It follows, then, that when you solve these challenges, you create happy users, and happy users will seek your solution over and over again. This pure definition of adoption, at scale, drives the ROI that so many analytical solutions promise.

Water Seeks the Path of Least Resistance

Humans, like water, will often seek the path of least resistance. Many times this leads to solving problems with familiar techniques, cumbersome tools, and/or manual steps. Without new ideas and new approaches, old and familiar ways of doing things can stay significantly entrenched in your organization and hobble innovation. What feels familiar is easy; conversely, change in processes or technologies often feels foreign and uncertain.

What was once your small, flowing stream can become a canyon of change for individuals—a canyon with stone banks keeps the river flowing in the same direction regardless of what is happening in the rest of the environment.

> By taking a human-centered approach, you first seek to understand the ultimate destination for users—as people.

What if this steam of flowing water met soft sand? The low friction sand would quickly give way and the stream would be diverted into a new direction. This new direction could be a faster path to the ultimate destination and could provide additional benefits along the way.

By taking a human-centered approach, you first seek to understand the ultimate destination for users—as people—and the organization and you survey the land for low-friction areas that channel water to provide maximum benefit and get you to your end state. In all of this, it's critical to remember that applications are designed for real humans, who need to get a job done. It is really that simple. The interaction with data and analytics needs to be as friction-free as possible, so that there are compelling reasons to engage. The process needs to allow individuals to spot, assess, and solve problems that are important to them.

Also, recognize that the bar is higher than it has ever been for how problems can be solved through technology. Look no further than your phone. Why have some apps remained, and some been archived to the store never to meet your fingertips again? The likely reason is that these go-to apps solve specific problems for you quickly. Larger technology solutions need to meet this requirement. Solutions need to be as friction-free as possible by meeting you where you are, both in form factor, as well as usability.

By understanding what works for specific individuals, in their environment, you can begin to design solutions that work for them.

Culture Eats Strategy for Lunch

Understanding what works for users can be tricky without a multifaceted approach. Environments in which analytics are deployed often have technical, political, and cultural considerations that can influence the short- and long-term adoption of analytical programs. The best analytics strategy in the world will be eaten for lunch if you don't have a solid understanding of each of these considerations.

From a cognitive design or human-centered engineering perspective, there are several disciplines you can leverage to ensure you have a complete understanding of the challenges your users face. Primary research is often the most basic and simply involves asking individuals specific open-ended questions that begin to reveal the goals, needs, and tasks they are looking to accomplish. Digging deeper in this space can reveal specific emotions or moments of truth that may provide tangible opportunities for analytics or other technologies to solve.

Observational research complements primary research in that people may not always do what they say or say what they do. Through observation "in the wild" you can augment the knowledge gained in more formal user interviews and probe more deeply with questions like, "Can you tell me why you did that?"

It's important to always be on the lookout for clues that, when put together, tell the complete story of the jobs that the system you're building needs to help end-users complete. Through this deep understanding and laying bare the end-to-end process, the real moments of truth, and their concomitant emotional needs states, the foundation is laid for sustained end-user adoption of the analytics solution you're striving to create.

Another important byproduct of this work is a clear understanding of the degree of change the new system may introduce to end users. This information should be used to construct specific change management and training programs to ensure that end users understand everything, from how change ladders, to overall corporate strategy, to the foundational "what's in it for me?"

The role of the champion begins to take shape about this time. The work of understanding the user perspective equips him or her with the knowledge and insight of not only the outcomes we are solving for, but also the ability to translate that insight to the specific end users and to communicate to them an understanding of why the inevitable change will benefit them personally. Ongoing communication becomes important at this stage because analytics programs will vary in duration, and the upfront empathy and research will ensure that consistency and relevance is maintained throughout the development process.

> Once you've taken the time to fully explore the opportunities and specific needs of individual end users, you can begin to construct rich and meaningful stories.

Tell a Story That Surprises Them

Stories are one of the most impactful ways to teach and explain situations or objectives. Storytelling goes back to ancient times and is incredibly powerful in the context of cognitive design.

Once you've taken the time to fully explore the opportunities and the specific needs of individual end users, you can begin to construct rich and meaningful stories. At this stage, user personas take shape and are a direct reflection of the interviews and observational research that has been performed. In addition, these users' journeys can be described in detail with the moments of truth becoming increasingly clear. These make-or-break moments are front and center and become self-evident to the audience. They can see clearly what needs to either be removed, improved, or extended.

The end goal is to both define and fall in love with the problem. One of the simplest and clearest tests to determine if you are on the right track at this stage is to be able to construct the following statement based on the person or personas you are trying to help:

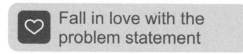

♡ Fall in love with the problem statement

[USER] wants to/needs to, but surprisingly …

Figure 5.1

The end word "surprisingly" is the hook and the point to which the collective creative energy of the project can be directed to create a solution that is meaningful emotionally for users, as well as beneficial for the organization.

Think Big/Dream Big

At this point in the design process, you've defined challenges that are preventing adoption by specific users. You should have confirmed with them that these indeed represent problems that, when solved, can result in individual and organizational benefit. Now is the time to get the creative juices flowing

There are several techniques that you can leverage, but the single most important element is to include several different perspectives on how the problem could be solved. Notice the word "could" versus "can." The important distinction is that, at this point, it's necessary to encourage extremely divergent thinking to elicit as many ideas as possible that could lead to a solution. Why? Because the danger is narrowing in on a particular technology or approach too soon in the process and limiting the outcomes you seek. Even more powerfully, divergent thinking may lead to transformative ideas that could change the nature of how your organization actually does business.

Divergent thinking is encouraged by ensuring that different roles or disciplines are "in the room" during problem-solving exercises. The most effective collaborations include people who are predominately left-brained, predominately right-brained, and a little bit of both. Also, their diverse professional disciplines may allow them to think about the same problem very differently. For example, a graphic designer will think about problems very differently from a solution architect. The key is to create an environment where every participant can build upon each other's ideas—and generate lots of them.

In this process, structured activities allow teams to generate volumes of ideas in a short amount of time and prioritize those that hit the sweet spot of end user needs, business viability, and technical viability. There will always be tradeoffs, but fully exploring the opportunity space will allow you to maximize the intersection.

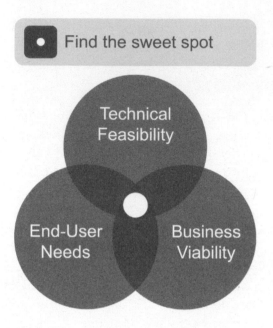

Figure 5.2

Fail Fast

Failing fast is a clichéd, but important, concept. As you look to drive end user adoption, the ability to quickly iterate through end user experiences and interactions, along with the data and analytics that will support it, is critical. It's essential to have the ability to test and validate ideas quickly, with real end users to ensure that the proposed solution, as it takes shape, does indeed solve the problem. It's not uncommon to iterate several times to get to the optimal solution, but if you employ cost-effective techniques like storyboards, wireframes, high-fidelity mockups, and clickable prototypes to validate a solution, it's quicker and easier to iterate.

> When designing end-user experiences, it's essential to consider the evolution of human interaction: from voice, to gesture, to touch.

Also, when designing end-user experiences, it's essential to consider the evolution of human interaction: from voice, to gesture, to touch. Form factors may also change the experience for a single-user persona—for example, from wearable, to mobile, to workstation. Accessibility considerations for color and sight need to be incorporated as well. A library of design patterns and assets that can readily be reassembled and reused can also help accelerate through multiple designs.

These storyboards, wireframes, and prototypes must be put into the hands of the end users and stakeholders as quickly as possible. Encourage your team members to embrace the notion that elements will be incorrect or out of place, and will need to be revised as the team moves to development. Early iteration cycles reduce rework, further solidify the outcomes, and validate that the solution will work for end uses. Prototypes and demos can be mockups or developed with just enough code to ensure technical viability.

In addition, a library of solution accelerators and microservices can also speed the realization of a solution. These highly malleable frameworks and components should have multiple use case applications. Like building models with LEGO® bricks when you were young, you can assemble components in multiple, diverse ways to produce different vehicles to achieve various outcomes.

Change management and training become important at this point in the process. Through both direct observation and feedback, you can tailor change management and training plans to accommodate what you learn from users' interactions with the solution design.

A few key questions to answer might include:

- Is the solution addressing both emotional and functional needs?
- Do first-time users understand what to do?
- How dramatically are we changing their process or workflow?
- Will users require additional coaching or training to achieve the outcome?

Asking questions like this will help change management and training teams develop and execute their plans in parallel with the technical development team. Engaging these teams early in the definition process can help you develop a solution that achieves the business outcomes you expect now, and will provide long-term ROI.

PUTTING IT TOGETHER

In the end, the solution design you develop serves as a clearly defined end state for development estimations as well as internal stakeholder alignment. To sum it up, from a body of work perspective, you will have:

- Definition on the business outcomes you're delivering
- Clarity on the specific users/personas that will deliver these business outcomes
- An understanding of your users' end-to-end needs: emotional, functional, and technical
- A clear vision of the end-to-end solution through storyboards, wireframes, prototypes, and/or demos

COGNITIVE DESIGN—THE HUMAN FACTOR IN PERVASIVE INTELLIGENCE

As we discussed, intelligence has a large human component. Pervasive data intelligence isn't simply about the information that comes from analytics systems. It's about understanding what information is useful to the people who rely on it and providing that information—that intelligence—to the right people, at the right time, in the right way.

Through the cognitive design process, you can achieve pervasive intelligence because you have a clear vision of the solution. You can use that vision to build a solution that drives high-impact outcomes. Pulling all the pieces together, you can also ensure that the nexus between user needs, business outcomes, and technical feasibility is maximized—well before costly development or investment occurs.

CHAPTER 6

You Are Only as Good as Your Data

Technically elegant, highly usable applications that give users the answers they need, when they need them, are a must for making data intelligence pervasive and driving high-impact outcomes. However, these applications will only be as good as the data that powers them. It won't matter how elegant or responsive an analytics system is—if the data isn't clean or reliable—users won't trust it, and they won't use it. Therefore, it's critical to eliminate data silos, secure and govern your data, and demand accountability for data governance (DG), throughout the enterprise. With a solid DG foundation to support your analytics efforts, you can embed intelligence in your organization to drive information yield; glean better insights; and enable faster, more accurate decision-making.

1 Consolidate data

- Get rid of data silos
- Consolidate to the cloud, a hybrid environment, or at least a common data store on premises—and create borderless data

2 Secure and govern

- Develop data governance policies that ensure clean, standardized data
- Secure data by implementing masking, encryption, and role-based access

3 Get the right tools

- Build a scalable, flexible architecture that grows and changes with your needs
- Invest in cutting-edge data visualization tools that are easy to use to facilitate collaboration and idea generation

Figure 6.1

CONSOLIDATE DATA

Fragmentation in systems and data hobbles efforts at enterprise-wide analysis and creates an environment where there is no single version of the truth about organizational data. The remedy for this is data consolidation to get rid of organizational silos. To be successful at using analytics, you must have a common (or federated) data store with clean, standardized data that provides the same answers to the same questions. That is, it creates borderless data.

More and more, companies are turning to the cloud (see Chapter 3 for a full discussion) to help them consolidate their data. The cloud provides a comprehensive, highly secure, and always-available platform for data storage that grows as you do and gives you the flexibility to store and access your data—both structured and unstructured—when you need it.

SECURE AND GOVERN

It's also crucial to have good data security and governance, especially when you're developing a borderless data environment. Clear and enforced data governance policies and procedures, as well as strong data security, are paramount. Data masking and encryption are fundamental security strategies, implementing role-based access. If you do it right, sound data governance can drive business agility by giving the right people the right access to the clean data they need, when they need it, and it can ameliorate concerns about data falling into the wrong hands.

THE RISING NEED FOR A CHIEF DATA OFFICER

As DG takes on a more prominent role, and as data volume, variety, and velocity increase, many companies are creating pathways of accountability for good data throughout the organization. Many leading companies have created a new role in the C-suite—the chief data officer (CDO).

Is there really room in the C-suite for one more person—especially one whose only concern is data? Maybe not 10 years ago, but there is today. CIOs (chief information officers) have their plates full with organizational strategy, data security, and overall analytics implementation. Data governance work is mired in the muck of technology and politics, and with the volume and types of data that need to be governed, the process of DG needs a dedicated leader.

Data governance is primarily concerned with making sure that data is consolidated, standardized, and governed across the enterprise. It's also process-oriented. One of its critical mandates is to overcome cultural and territorial boundaries and put policies and procedures in place that ensure that the organizational data, no matter the system it resides in, is high quality and provides a "single version of the truth" to anyone who accesses it. For that to happen, someone needs to take accountability for the impact that good—or bad—data has on the organization.

> A critical data governance mandate is to overcome cultural and territorial boundaries and put policies and procedures in place that ensure that the organizational data, no matter the system it resides in, is high quality and provides a "single version of the truth" to anyone who accesses it.

That's where the CDO comes in. Under a CDO, the DG function can garner the visibility, budget, and resources to meet its mandate. Additionally, a CDO can provide the strategic guidance to the DG process to steer the effort through choppy political waters that decentralized DG efforts cannot.

So, yes, it's always a good idea to think before you split executive responsibilities and add yet another direct report to the CEO, but in this case—because data is such a valuable strategic, yet complex, asset—the CDO position becomes mandatory.

PERVASIVE INTELLIGENCE AND DATA GOVERNANCE

It may seem a stretch to pair pervasive intelligence with a procedure-oriented discipline like data governance, but really, it's not. It's actually a simple equation. To be intelligent and survive—much less thrive—any organism, including companies that function like living entities, must have accurate information to make decisions. A robust data governance gives you the accurate information you need to enable that pervasive intelligence.

CHAPTER **7**

The Data Security Awakening

I f your company is like most others, you face a dilemma. To maximize information value and use that information to make data intelligence pervasive throughout your organization, you must make that data available to employees, business partners, and customers. However, without limiting how many times—and with who—information is viewed, copied, transmitted, and analyzed, appropriately controlling access to data is difficult.

As a result, your proprietary data is often scattered throughout the organization, and among affiliate entities, which increases the chance that some or all of it will wind up in the wrong hands. The only way you can avoid this problem is to implement in-depth defensive strategies to protect your most valuable, sensitive data.

DATA SECURITY: A QUESTION OF MANAGING RISK

Implementing effective data security is predicated on understanding how an organization can effectively solve the problem of providing appropriate access while limiting unauthorized access. You can begin the process asking five simple questions:

1. What are the information assets you possess that require protection?

2. Where do these assets reside within your enterprise ecosystems?

3. Which security and privacy controls are needed to protect these assets?

4. Who has access to these assets, and is that access necessary for them to do their job?

5. Is logging and monitoring done to help detect and prevent unauthorized access to these assets?

If your organization honestly answers these questions, you can begin to assess your security condition and implement an enterprise security strategy and architecture. The primary point to keep in mind is that security implementation must always be carried out with risk as the primary factor in determining strategy. Therefore, during strategy development and architecture review, it's essential to use an authoritative framework to implement best practices and measure conformity to those practices.

A primary point to keep in mind is that security implementation must always be carried out with risk as the primary factor in determining strategy.

Evaluate any security mechanisms and controls you implement based on the following criteria:

- The likelihood of damage if the control is weak, ineffective, or nonexistent
- The inherent economic impact of a successful cyberattack
- The completeness and effectiveness of a remediating control

This information will help you identify and quantify risk. Once you've completed this process, the identified high risks in the security architecture can be mitigated to an acceptable level.

Understanding the Value of Data Security

Answering the five questions posed earlier is only the first step in understanding the sensitive data lifecycle. After you've answered the questions, you must analyze the answers, identify or acquire human and technical resources to implement data security, and leverage those resources to deliver outcomes that provide tangible risk-mitigation value.

Failing to fund and implement a monetarily expensive data-encryption program to protect customer or regulated data at rest is a very poor exercise in frugality.

Strategies that mitigate risk involve more than hurling expensive technology at perceived security risks. Instead, they are concerned with the identification of the sensitive data that needs protection—as well as where and when to protect that data. If you don't know what to protect, and where it resides, you will waste critical funding without addressing the real issues you face.

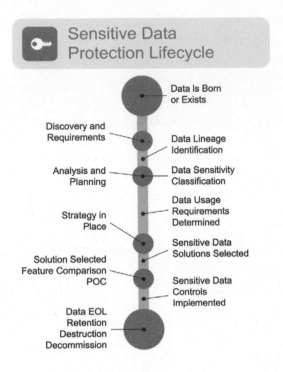

Figure 7.1

Therefore, it's essential to understand the value of data, across its lifecycle, before devising and implementing data security solutions. For example, low value, nonregulated data doesn't usually present a good use case for encryption or other expensive control solutions. The cost benefit equation just doesn't work here. In contrast, failing to fund and implement a monetarily expensive data-encryption program to protect customer or regulated data at rest is a very poor exercise in frugality. Why? Because the cumulative cost of notifying customers of a subsequent data breach will far exceed the costs of implementing the security solution to prevent the breach.

Let's look at a simple example. Say we have an expected loss of $700 million from a breach of 70 million unencrypted records.* However, if we encrypt the data, it will cost approximately $2 million to

---

* Breach notification, remediation, fortification, brand damage, and other economic harm is calculated at just $10 per record. This may be appropriate for bank records, but healthcare records run $100–$400 each.

encrypt those 70 million records. The benefits of encryption are clear, in the form of a $698 million savings if we encrypt—not to mention the intangible benefit of avoiding incurring a reputational loss that might be incalculable—and unrecoverable.

National and International Data Security Protections

In the past decade, many countries have taken significant legislative and regulatory action to force companies to secure their—and their customers'—data. You may not think of your company as a global concern, so you might not see the value in learning about international data security measures. However, if you engage in eCommerce, if you source parts for any product, or if you work with vendor partners who do, you might be at risk of violating data security measures outside the United States.

The General Data Protection Regulation and the California Consumer Privacy Act

The General Data Protection Regulation (GDPR) 2016/679 is a European Union (EU) regulation concerning data protection and privacy for all people who reside within the EU, and within its concomitant European Economic Area. In the United States, the California Consumer Privacy Act of 2018 (CCPA) is also designed to enact sweeping protections for personal information and privacy.

CCPA is stricter than GDPR in some areas but not in others. CCPA sets up an opt-in system governing data sources, uses, and categories. Like GDPR, consumers are in most cases required to consent to data collection by businesses. Many exceptions exist. CCPA also contains a right to be forgotten and of portability much like GDPR. Also, age restrictions not seen in GDPR exist in CCPA. Enforcement penalties depend on the nature and extent of damages. Private suits are authorized for some violations but not others, with exceptions.

As with GDPR, CCPA has multiple requirements for establishing strong privacy practices and adequate technical security safeguards (controls). You can effectively address these requirements by conducting a security assessment, control implementation, and remediation.

New York State

In 2017, the New York Legislature passed 23 NYCRR Part 500, a set of comprehensive data protection regulations that, in part, mandate that each company that does business in the state, or with residents that live in New York state, must:

> Design a program that addresses its risks in a robust fashion. Senior management must take this issue seriously and be responsible for the organization's cybersecurity program,…. confirming [annual] compliance…. [This] program must ensure the safety and soundness of the institution and protect its customers…. It is critical for all regulated institutions … to move swiftly and urgently to adopt a cybersecurity program…. The number of cyber events has been steadily increasing and estimates of potential risk to our financial services industry are stark.

China

Finally, even though you may not know it, your company may have a tangential relationship or interaction with Chinese companies or products. Therefore, it's essential to understand the China Cyber Security Law (June 1, 2018) and China Information Security Standard (May 1, 2018).

The new Chinese data protection law mandates requirements such as the opt-in of all Chinese citizens before data can be stored or processed about them (excepting the Chinese government) and imposes stiff penalties for removing data from the country on Chinese citizens without the explicit consent of the citizen and the Chinese government—and for removing certain data types from the country at all, based on its relationship to Chinese national security. These laws also apply to certain business data.

This section only scratches the surface of these protective regulations. The bottom line is that more and more municipalities, states, and countries are enacting some form of data protection measures to combat cybercrime and protect their citizens. You must take great care to understand the laws and regulations that apply to your business domain. If you don't, the result could be catastrophic.

ENTERPRISE RISK ASSESSMENT CHECKLIST

- ☐ Appoint a chief information security officer (CISO) and staff to establish cybersecurity program and policy.
- ☐ Maintain confidentiality, integrity, and availability of nonpublic information.
- ☐ Encrypt nonpublic information in transit and at rest unless infeasible and CISO approved compensating controls in place.
- ☐ Conduct an annual penetration test and biannual vulnerability assessment.
- ☐ Implement multifactor authentication if indicated by a risk assessment.
- ☐ Establish access requirements.
- ☐ Practice proper application security.
- ☐ Insure a forensic audit trail of data processing.
- ☐ Secure data disposal eliminating unneeded data retention (data minimization).
- ☐ Train and monitor users.
- ☐ Document incident management policy with a 72-hour breach notification process.
- ☐ Require third-party service provider security policy based on its own risk assessment.

PERVASIVE INTELLIGENCE AND DATA SECURITY

Part of being an intelligent organization—of making data intelligence pervasive—is understanding the value of your information and appropriately distributing that information to the people who need it to make decisions, without letting it fall into the hands of people who don't. As a result, data security—and compliance with the complex assortment of global data security regulations—will be critical in your ability to make intelligence pervasive. If people don't have access to the information they need, and your information infrastructure is insecure, in addition to being vulnerable to cyberattacks, your intelligence efforts will suffer, and your ability to achieve those game-changing outcomes will be severely compromised.

PART II

Technology to Achieve Pervasive Intelligence

The technology you choose to implement analytics plays a critical role in helping you achieve pervasive intelligence and realize game-changing outcomes. To embed intelligence into your organizational DNA, it's essential to have a data architecture that supports many different tool types, flexible and scalable to change and grow with you as your analysis needs change. It's also crucial to have tools that are easy to use, and that have excellent visualization capabilities, enabling end users to access and interpret data without having to be data scientists themselves.

New technologies are revolutionizing the analytics space. Technologies such as data lakes—which enable cheaper storage and faster access and analysis of unstructured data—help companies deal with the flood of data that threatens to drown them but provides little information. Artificial intelligence—especially machine learning—takes today's predictive and prescriptive analytics to a new level and enables true digital transformation.

What's more is that companies that get analytics right will embed intelligence into their operations—into their organization's DNA—so that analytics is not just a series of spot projects, but an industrialized process that enables a consistent approach to analytical development and problem-solving. With this AnalyticOps approach, analytics will be an integral part of the fabric of the organization, not just something it does.

Finally, intelligent clouds couple the transformative power of cloud computing with the ability to place analytics capabilities in the cloud. With intelligent clouds, companies are able to ramp up their analytics power when they need it. They are also able to access the latest and most powerful technologies, to make data intelligence pervasive and achieve their high-impact outcomes.

CHAPTER **8**

The Evolution of Data Lakes as a Fundamental Part of a New Ecosystem Architecture

ervasive intelligence requires an intelligent, reliable information architecture. The foundation of an intelligent information architecture is the enterprise data warehouse (DW)—or at a minimum, function-oriented DWs that rely on the same governance structure and data definitions. Traditional DW implementations follow a set approach: define the requirements, identify (structured) data sources, define the schema, load and format the data, then distribute the data through presentation layers.

You can use historical transaction or event data in your DW to figure out what happened and why it might have happened. Based on available data, you can form hypotheses and test them against the data in the warehouse to either confirm or refute your suspicions. It can democratize BI (business intelligence) and put the power of analysis in the hands of less-than-tech-savvy users, presenting them with a single version of the "truth," no matter who's asking.

CHANGES IN DATA DICTATE CHANGES IN STORAGE TECHNOLOGY

Data warehouses work well as long as the data fits what you've defined, but no one needs to tell you that the nature of data has changed significantly over the past decade. The volume of unstructured and streaming data has far surpassed that of traditional, structured data. That flood has given rise to a new repository: the data lake.

Data lakes store unstructured data and format it when it's queried, to enable broader and deeper data exploration by data scientists. Raw data is ingested—either in batches or in real time—and stored in its native format. The data is curated by capturing metadata, but it's only formatted on read. That is, when someone wants to retrieve the data. Because much of the technology is open source and the processing at load time is less, data lakes are also cost-effective.

Data lakes also enable a different analytical process. Instead of forming a hypothesis and testing it against the data, you build analysis "sandboxes" where data scientists can use sophisticated modeling techniques to parse the data to spot trends and patterns. In essence, the data scientist uses a model to make an observation or spot a pattern, then forms a hypothesis. It's kind of backwards to the EDW (enterprise data warehouse) analysis approach, but it's complementary.

Advantages of Data Lakes

Data lakes—for all their documented pitfalls—enable the fastest, most flexible platform for analytics data delivery. Unlike data warehouses, data lakes ingest data—of virtually all types—in its native form, and only upon query by the user is that data formatted for analysis. Data lakes also typically use open-source storage technology such as Hadoop, so the storage costs are greatly reduced.

> Data lakes support traditional technical functionality such as cleansing and governance, and their structure—organization and formatting when the user queries the data, rather than on entry into the data lake—enables flexible, deep analysis using multiple data types simultaneously.

Data lakes also support traditional technical functionality such as cleansing and governance, and their structure—organization and formatting when the user queries the data, rather than on entry into the data lake—enables flexible, deep analysis using multiple data types simultaneously.

Maybe the most important advantage of a data lake, however, is its speed to deployment. Data lakes—because the data is ingested in its native format, and because the storage is open source—can be developed and deployed much more quickly than a data warehouse, delivering better business outcomes faster and cheaper.

Although they deliver powerful results, data lakes really only have three processes: data ingestion, preparation, and discovery.

Ingestion

For data ingestion, most data lake technologies support batch loads of data. However, for near real-time analysis, what's needed is a data lake product that supports both batch and streaming data ingestion in virtually any format. With this capability, analysts can query the system and get data that has almost zero latency, thus helping them ask and answer questions and make decisions that have an almost immediate impact on the business.

Preparation

The preparation process is where native-format data that has been ingested into the data lake is transformed—based on previously set policies and rules—into usable data that can be queried for analysis. Best-in-class data lake technologies help you create rules to standardize and validate data based on your unique business rules and analysis goals—along with any regulations you might have to observe.

For instance, an insurance company may need to mask sensitive data such as social security numbers, based on user needs and security roles. A top-notch data lake product will also have prebuilt transformation algorithms for common data types. This will speed up the transformation process and deliver data into users' hands more quickly.

Discovery

The data discovery process is where the benefits of a data lake are most apparent. In a data lake, there is an enormous pool of cleansed data, just waiting to be accessed and analyzed. In choosing a data lake technology, you'll want to look for an intuitive graphical user interface (GUI) that helps users search for the data they want and helps them build queries that return data in a graphics or text-based format that supports sophisticated analysis.

Clear Benefits

The benefits of a data lake are clear:

- They're quick to deploy. Because data lakes use schema on read (which means that data isn't processed until its queried), there isn't a months-long effort to write a rigid schema to organize the data. Instead, data is only organized when users need to access it.

- They're flexible and scalable. Because they accept most data types and they're open source to facilitate more storage, data lakes can change as your organization changes, and they can grow as you grow.

- They make managing data easy. With powerful cleansing and transformation capabilities facilitated through an easy-to-use interface—as well as prebuilt transformation rules—data lakes make data management less complex and more streamlined.

- They deliver powerful analysis capabilities. With user-friendly GUIs and self-service data query abilities, users can quickly search for and access the data they need, and ask business-driven, complex questions—driving more informed, quicker decision-making that leads to accelerated outcomes.

DATA LAKES AND PERVASIVE INTELLIGENCE

The volume and variety of data that inundates companies today is growing exponentially. It's essential to have data storage methods that enable you to store multiple data types for access—when and where you need it. Data lakes are the answer for all that unstructured data that DWs can't handle. And again, the equation is straightforward. More data equals better intelligence available to more people to facilitate quicker, better decision-making and achievement of those outcomes that have the greatest impact on your long-term success—that is, pervasive intelligence.

CHAPTER 9

Artificial Intelligence and Machine Learning— The Future of Pervasive Intelligence

Most companies today have fairly good predictive—and maybe even prescriptive—capabilities that provide them with deeper, more timely insights into their business performance. Those insights are driving better decisions and helping make your operations more efficient. However, predictive analytics is the ante these days.

Leading companies have begun to realize that artificial intelligence (AI) is the technology that will take their analytics to the next, very powerful level, enabling them to embed intelligence at the cellular level of the organization.

Artificial intelligence—in the way it's being used in this discussion—can also be used synonymously with cognitive computing. While there's really no agreed-on definition of AI, here it is defined as hardware and/or software that simulates human thinking.

AI has three fundamental characteristics:

1. It learns as information changes, even in real time.
2. It can understand data in contextual terms, and it can help you interact—or can interact on its own—with users, using that contextual information.
3. It is curious. It remembers previous events and asks questions, returns answers, and makes recommendations based on those events.

THE POWER OF (ARTIFICIAL) INTELLIGENCE

AI brings tremendous, transformative power to those companies that embed it into their organizational intelligence infrastructures. It can transform your analytics capabilities and give you a competitive edge that helps drive value by changing the way you operate, the way you make decisions, and the way you view and interact with your customers.

It Changes the Way You Operate

With AI, you can transform your traditional supply chain into a digital supply network (DSN) that is connected, smart, scalable, and flexible.

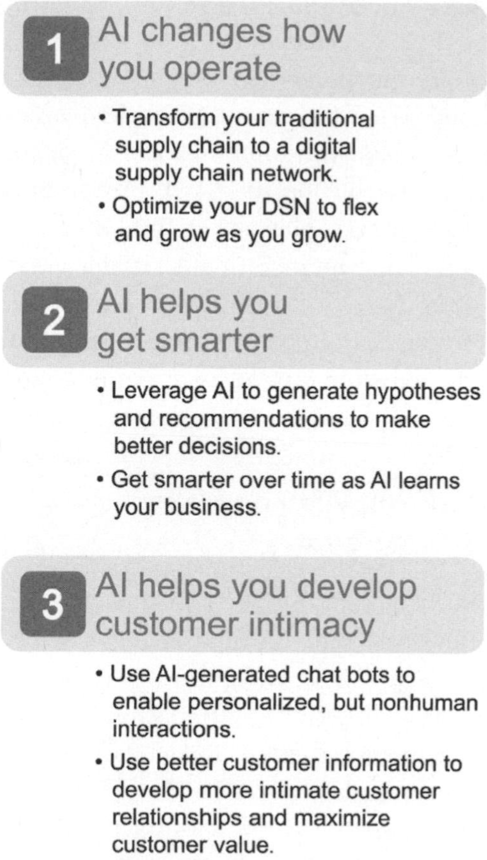

1 **AI changes how you operate**

- Transform your traditional supply chain to a digital supply chain network.
- Optimize your DSN to flex and grow as you grow.

2 **AI helps you get smarter**

- Leverage AI to generate hypotheses and recommendations to make better decisions.
- Get smarter over time as AI learns your business.

3 **AI helps you develop customer intimacy**

- Use AI-generated chat bots to enable personalized, but nonhuman interactions.
- Use better customer information to develop more intimate customer relationships and maximize customer value.

Figure 9.1

You can use that intelligence to drive coordinated planning, 24/7 connections with suppliers and customers, smart production models, and dynamic logistics operations that can help you adjust quickly, as your needs change.

DSNs are highly adaptable, interwoven—almost organic—ecosystems that help you optimize the operation of your production processes and your relationships with suppliers. They help you maximize the value of every step in your product and workflow to deliver the right products to the right people, at the right time.

It Changes the Way You Make Decisions

AI uses information much like the human brain. It draws on experience (information, past and present) to make connections and form hypotheses. It can make recommendations based on that information—and it can adjust on the fly, based on the new information it receives. Your decisions will be smarter and faster.

What's truly transformative is that AI-enabled systems get smarter over time, as they couple the past with the present to create an environment for contextual learning that continuously evolves and improves to deliver better long-term insights and decision-making capabilities.

It Changes How You View and Interact with Your Customers

Customers today—especially those ultravaluable millennials—want a plethora of channels available for interaction. The phone is dead. Yet they also want a deeply personal—intimate—relationship with retailers and service providers. AI hits the sweet spot. Chat bots—think Siri or Alexa—are revolutionizing customer service. In customer service, chat bots—even if they don't employ voice capabilities—use AI to facilitate "personalized" customer contact while freeing up actual humans to handle deeper or more complex issues.

AI can also leverage previous information about customer interactions to predict current and future needs and can offer "smart" suggestions for services, offers, or promotions that are individualized for particular customers. With such individualized information, you can create a deeply intimate relationship with your customers that builds extreme loyalty and maximizes customer value, both now and in the future.

AI IN PRACTICE

But how does AI look in practice? The future of AI across all industries is bright, but in this section, we'll look at how using AI helps companies in the finance and insurance, retail, and supply-chain/manufacturing sectors transform the way they do business.

What's truly transformative is that AI-enabled systems get smarter over time, as they couple the past with the present to create an environment for contextual learning that continuously evolves and improves to deliver better long-term insights and decision-making capabilities.

The Future of AI in Finance and Insurance

In the future, instead of chatting with a customer service representative, you'll chat with a bot that has natural language processing capabilities and is armed with tons of customer specific interaction data that will mimic the human-to-human chatting capabilities available today.

AI will also enhance security and market analysis capabilities. Biometric data such as face, voice, or even retinal recognition will become the norm for security measures. And investment banks and hedge funds will use AI to perform deep analysis to better understand the human and social factors that influence markets and use that sentiment analysis to make better decisions.

AI in Retail

In the next half decade, retailers will use AI to make predictions about inventory needs and adjust levels in real time. These systems will make suggestions to store managers about which items to order, and in some cases, companies may enable them to make purchases without human intervention.

Product placement will also get a boost from AI. Gaze detection technologies will be used to analyze customer interest and place products in ways that optimize foot traffic patterns and visual attention. These systems will also analyze that foot traffic and direct product placement based on not just seasonal, but demographic trends such as age, gender, and so on. The thinking will go something like this: older women tend to shop on Thursday mornings, so we'll put products of interest to them in high-traffic areas on Thursdays.

Another obvious trend for AI augmentation will be in loss prevention. Detection of customers (and employees) exhibiting suspicious behavior will be made easier by algorithms that leverage big data to better understand behavior patterns. Care is needed here, however, to scrupulously avoid inappropriate profiling at all costs.

AI in Manufacturing/Supply Chain

Over the next 5 to 10 years, AI will also revolutionize the business for large logistics companies and manufacturers. AI will be used to eliminate many manual processes now handled by humans: invoice exception tracking, responses to inquiries, purchase order corrections, and so on. Think how much this could free up employees to engage in productive tasks.

Other leading companies will use chat bots (see "The Future of AI in Finance and Insurance" earlier) to engage with suppliers in routine communications, place purchase orders, monitor regulatory compliance vis-à-vis materials, and to keep up with the voluminous documentation that often bedevils—and slows down—logistics operations.

Another obvious application of AI (and one that syncs well with retail) that will become prevalent is inventory forecasting: correlating supply with demand and optimizing decision-making processes with intelligent algorithms and machine-learning-augmented analysis of big data.

MACHINE LEARNING—THE STAR OF ARTIFICIAL INTELLIGENCE

How will this AI-augmented future arrive? For many use cases, it will arrive packaged in machine-learning algorithms. As more sophisticated, easy-to-use analytics tools have hit the market in the past five years, self-service analytics implementations have skyrocketed. These self-service capabilities take some of the pressure off IT staffs to produce, and they've created a new generation of citizen data scientists, but it's a double-edged sword.

> Machine learning algorithms will serve to augment analysts' knowledge and enrich their understanding of their decision-making environment, spanning departments and functions. This will take place across the analytics continuum from data preparation, to analysis, to insight, to action.

As data volumes become larger and more complex, erstwhile data scientists are often overwhelmed by the process. Increasingly, decisions require cross-functional knowledge, and the number of variables that drive decision-making and actionable insights is multiplied almost exponentially. As a result, business people acting as analysts often fall back on their biases and only explore the hypotheses they started with. Thus, they're likely to miss key insights that may go against their biases or hypotheses. When that happens, decision-making is hampered by incomplete or faulty information, and the analytics effort suffers.

Enter machine learning. Machine learning algorithms will serve to augment analysts' knowledge and enrich their understanding of their decision-making environment, spanning departments and functions. This will take place across the analytics continuum from data preparation, to analysis, to insight, to action.

Augmented analytics and data preparation will enable "smart" data discovery that will eliminate, or greatly reduce, bias in decision-making via an impartial view of the data and the results produced from such an analysis. The result? A virtuous cycle of increased trust in the analytics system, which leads to high user adoption rates (more people making better decisions). In turn, this leads to increased ROI (return on investment) via better decision-making and the ability to act more quickly on those decisions.

> The best of both worlds are hybrid algorithms that combine elements of both supervised and unsupervised learning methods to couple the relative certainty of supervised learning with the power and novel insight generation of unsupervised learning. One of these so-called hybrid models is reinforcement learning.

Machine Learning Algorithms

There are three general types of ML algorithms: supervised learning, unsupervised learning, and hybrid algorithms. Each has its place, depending on the task at hand, the data you have to feed the algorithm, and the outcomes you seek.

Supervised Learning

Supervised learning is the workhorse of ML. It involves training your machine with paired data—a series of inputs where the output is known. You feed the machine enough of these data pairs and it learns which data go together. For example, if you feed the machine information on the stock market, along with date and economic information, you can construct a relatively accurate predictive model. Of course, it won't be 100% accurate. For example, humans run the stock market, so there's irrationality, and therefore unpredictability—but with enough time and data, it'll get really good at predicting the Dow Jones Average over time.

You can also build supervised learning models that classify things. For example, researchers can feed the machine population and epidemiological data and build a model of people who are likely to get cancer, heart disease, or diabetes. You can also build predictive models of customer segments that are likely to churn, demand forecasts, project outcomes, financial performance—the list goes on and on. The upshot is that if you can more accurately predict events or behaviors, you can devise and implement strategies to plan for, and capitalize, on them.

Unsupervised Learning

Unsupervised learning is the powerful wild card of ML. Its power is, unfortunately, sometimes hindered by its unpredictability and the difficulty in using it effectively. With unsupervised learning, the inputs are known, but the predicted outputs aren't. The machine learns by trial and error. Inputs and outputs are paired by experience. Given enough data and time, the algorithm shows you patterns in the data that you would never discover using supervised methods.

However, because the outputs aren't known in advance, it's often difficult to know whether the results of the model are valid. Clustering, the most common technique used for unsupervised learning, involves grouping set members with common traits together. For example, you can segment customers with similar buying habits or demographics. The difficulty lies in knowing if these groups provide useful insights, how many of them should exist, or whether they're even grouped correctly. You can refine the model over time, but there's always a level of uncertainty. If you can live with that, though, unsupervised models can provide unique and very valuable insights.

Hybrid Algorithms—The Best of Both Worlds

The best of both worlds are hybrid algorithms that combine elements of both supervised and unsupervised learning methods to couple the relative certainty of supervised learning with the power and novel insight generation of unsupervised learning. One of these so-called hybrid models is reinforcement learning. You might have heard of this type of algorithm if you've read about computers that have been trained to beat opponents at games like Pokemon go, Atari, and chess. Reinforcement learning algorithms basically pair observations and measurements to a prescribed set of actions in the process of trying to achieve and optimize a reward. The computer interacts with its environment in an attempt to learn how to master it.

The outcomes aren't known in advance, but desired ones are rewarded. Reinforcement learning can be applied to all sorts of business activities such as risk management, inventory management, logistics, product design. The list is huge. The bottom line is that reinforcement learning can help you discover optimal outcomes that you seek, and it can reveal outcomes that you didn't seek, but that you can leverage to optimize your operations.

Two Caveats

This discussion represents only a small scratch on the vast surface of ML. There are other techniques, such as anomaly detection to help detect fraud and bolster risk management efforts, that can help you improve your analytics and increase your bottom line. There are two caveats, however, when using any ML algorithm. One is that it's easy to introduce bias into ML algorithms, so you must constantly measure your results against your goals and ethics. Second, it takes a huge volume of clean data to achieve valid, predictable results with ML algorithms. If you keep those two caveats in mind, it's really a no-brainer decision to include ML capabilities into your analytics ecosystem.

OPTIMIZING MACHINE LEARNING EFFORTS

As we've seen, ML can boost your analytics efforts by helping computer systems learn, in a manner that simulates human learning. The technology you use to implement ML, however, is not nearly as important as the thought process behind your implementation.

Technically, ML is no different from any other analytics technology. There's a method to it: ingest the data into a data lake or other large data store, transform it for analysis, build and train a model, then refine that model to help it learn and provide more accurate data for analysis. Along the way, however, you'll run into pitfalls that have nothing to do with technology, but with how the technology is leveraged to gain a deeper understanding of the business, and how—and by whom—the goals for the ML initiative are defined.

There are a few steps you can take to ensure that your ML initiative gets off on the right footing and stays that way. This discussion focuses on ML, but it really applies to any analytics effort.

Let the Business Lead the Way

Technology is useless if it doesn't provide the outcomes you seek. Usually, when a tech project fails, it's not the fault of the technology itself. Rather, it's the fault of the people who defined the goals for it. As with any technology, the outcomes for your ML initiative should always be defined by the business. You can design and train the most intricate ML models, but they'll be useless if they don't provide the information that business owners need to do their jobs. Bottom line: actionable insights from ML/analytics initiatives can be gained only if the business leads the efforts.

Communicate the Power of the Technology

Again, the business must lead. Go all out on investing in the technologies you need to integrate ML in your analytics initiative. However, it is critical that business users understand the technology—not the nuts and bolts of the higher math behind it, but the general idea behind what you're trying to achieve technically, and how you're going about it at a high level. Communicate the power of the technology. Be a champion for it and stress the importance of the business objectives behind it, and how ML technology will enable you to meet them.

> You'll always have that person who says, "It can't be done; we don't operate that way. It'll be too hard to change." Don't buy it. You can do what you want, if you want it badly enough. Just because you haven't done it in the past doesn't mean you can't do it now. Trust the numbers and commit the resources you'll always have that person who says, "it can't be done; we don't operate that way. It'll be too hard to change." Don't buy it. You can do what you want, if you want it badly enough. Just because you haven't done it in the past doesn't mean you can't do it now. Trust the numbers and commit the resources.

Keep the Dream in Mind

The defining feature of ML technology is how it enhances the predictive capabilities of analytics tools. Combined with emerging prescriptive capabilities of leading analytics software, ML-enhanced analytics can provide you with a powerful roadmap for future success. However, as with any project, you'll always have that person who says, "It can't be done; we don't operate that way. It'll be too hard to change." Don't buy it. You can do what you want, if you want it badly enough. Just because you haven't done it in the past doesn't mean you can't do it now. Trust the numbers and commit the resources to make it happen.

Pair Technology and Humans for Optimal Outcomes

As a corollary, however, don't forget the human element. Although ML enables you to go beyond human understanding to get the insights you need to achieve better outcomes, humans still play a large part in any ML/analytics endeavor. The combination of human experience and ML-augmented insights will help you achieve optimal outcomes. Trust the numbers, to be sure, but also trust the human business users who have a deep knowledge of your markets, customers, products, and services. By capitalizing on the connection between humans and machines you can truly achieve the outcomes you seek—and move beyond them to optimized operations and market leadership.

AI AND PERVASIVE INTELLIGENCE

Traditional technology only goes so far. Intelligence that is innate and human-like will make the difference between those companies that thrive and those that merely survive—or worse. That intelligence must also be pervasive throughout the organization. AI and ML—which are really misnomers because they make your company's intelligence capabilities more human-like and sentient—are the foundation of that pervasive intelligence.

CHAPTER 10

Analytics Operations to Enable Pervasive Intelligence

Most people now realize the massive opportunity advanced analytics can unlock for business, that is, the ability to drive significant top- and bottom-line impacts and help embed intelligence capabilities throughout the organization. Untold companies have spent millions of dollars to build data science practices, as well as the associated analytics infrastructure to support them.

Business leaders often struggle to understand the value of data science, however, because they're unable to operationalize the insights they glean from their analytics/data science activities. At many companies, data science teams generate tremendous analytical insights, but they struggle to move those insights quickly from the data lab environment to production, at scale—in what might be thought of as an industrialized method. They can't reap intelligence from information and make that data intelligence pervasive.

Enter AnalyticOps—which combines processes and tools to address the gap from insight to pervasive intelligence and realized value. AnalyticOps is the "productionalization" of analytics: bringing analytics from theory and numbers to production and value. It is a systematic approach that drives automation, standardization, and governance to unlock the value inherent in your organization—and it does this at scale.

OPERATIONALIZING ANALYTICS

AnalyticOps sounds like a buzzword. Everyone talks about it even if they don't really understand what it entails, or how to do it. The mantra is to, "Just get it done." But what is "it?" What does it mean to operationalize analytics?

Operationalized analytics means having a sustainable, repeatable process to quickly deploy predictive and prescriptive analytics models throughout the organization—a mass-production model for analytics.

With the advent of evermore-sophisticated analytics tools, coupled with the deluge of unstructured data, this mass-production model development capability quickly becomes mandatory in deploying successful analytics solutions.

Truly operationalized analytics has a few critical characteristics:

1. Good data and governance
2. An iterative, business-led development ecosystem
3. Self-service capabilities that fit all (or most) users

Figure 10.1

Good Data

If someone asks you the name of the MLB club in Atlanta, and you say, "It's the Atlanta Braves," but you tell someone else who asks the same question that the team's name is the Hawks, *and* you tell a third person that it's the Jaguars, eventually people will catch on that your information is false and you're not trustworthy. It's the same with analytics systems. If people don't get the same answers to the same questions, they won't trust the system.

It is imperative to have consistent—and consistently good—data throughout your company's information repositories. Consistent data requires a strong governance initiative in place to ensure that policies are set and followed. The governance effort must also be empowered by, and accountable to, the C-suite.

An Iterative, Business-Led Development Ecosystem

The prime directive for pervasive data intelligence is to build systems that can flow to production quickly and drive faster, deeper insights into the business, thus enabling pervasive intelligence. These systems should be flexible enough to change with market conditions. To build flexible, reliable systems, you need the ability to develop and deploy models quickly, make the decision to move to production, and scale up or close and retrench.

The Proof of Concept

One accelerator to the deployment of a flexible intelligence model that drives business value is a proof of concept (PoC) project. For many companies, however, PoC has unfortunately become a synonym for failure or boondoggle. PoCs have earned their reputation because sometimes they provide only incremental advances—and thus limited value. Instead, PoCs should be viewed as a true first step on the path to a real production system.

Skilled analytical resources must collaborate with data engineering teams in a PoC so that the path to production is well-defined and milestones are developed and met. With well-defined milestones and proper management, and with an eye towards putting the PoC into production, instead of incremental advancements, the PoC can truly provide a window into how well a future successful analytics model might help you solve your most pressing issues.

> AnalyticOps is about creating sustainable data products. Following this best practice framework can accelerate projects in the early stages and fast-track the realization of their value to the business.

A Development Framework

Whether you are investing into a PoC or a full-fledged analytics engagement, a proper, robust framework is critical to help you to build repeatable models for analytics deployment. By standardizing on

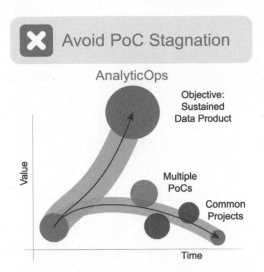

Figure 10.2

a framework, you can build analytic ecosystems to develop, deploy, consume, and scale in an iterative cycle.

As you deploy analytics models, the framework you choose should give you the capability to monitor and manage performance to ensure consistent performance and alert you when problems arise. AnalyticOps is about creating sustainable data products. Following this best practice framework can accelerate projects in the early stages and fast-track the realization of their value to the business.

Self-Service Analytics That Fit All (or Most) Users

Users come equipped with a variety of skills. Some are power users who have the confidence to develop the system themselves. Others are neophytes who need hand-holding to use any sort of analytics capabilities. Most users fall somewhere in between. Your analytics model-building environment must efficiently accommodate as many of these users as possible.

Self-service analytics is how a large, varied, user base can be supported. Your analytics framework should give users the ability to construct models and adjust those models based on results. Users can explore data, ask additional questions, and gain new insights based on results from different hypotheses fed into multiple models. It is a democratized sandbox where users can play on equal terms, regardless of their expertise, and can participate in the generation of new insights that help grow the bottom line.

EMBEDDING ANALYTICOPS THROUGHOUT THE ORGANIZATION

Unfortunately most analytics projects never make it out of the PoC state to enterprise deployment. That is a tremendous amount of wasted time, effort, and money. A big contributor to this failure on return is that analytics initiatives are often treated as projects: something the organization was "doing," not something the organization was "becoming."

After decades of analytical capability development, tool suites and methodologies have come and gone. Innumerable analytics theories have been offered and rejected. But a common thread for success is intelligence that is embedded at the operational level throughout the enterprise—intelligence that is pervasive.

The value of intelligence to the business can only be realized when analytics tools are running within existing production systems or business processes. These processes must function within the normal business operations and within the business's strategic framework. It sounds simple, and it's now cliché, but it's an axiom that's continually ignored: There can be no successful analytics initiative that is not intricately imbedded in the DNA of your company without AnalyticOps.

The AnalyticOps philosophy rests at the intersection of your company's data science, data engineering, and process engineering efforts. It is a mind-set more than a methodology. It's not about what tools to use or what principles and practices to follow, rather, it's about deploying analytics that fit your individual business needs.

Figure 10.3

AnalyticOps Differentiates Itself from Traditional Development

Although they are similar in high-level objectives, AnalyticOps differs from more traditional development approaches in a few key ways:

1. Development versus production
   a. Traditional: development and production "stack" are generally the same.
   b. AnalyticOps: model exploration and development are typically performed using large amounts of historical data to develop and test the models. However, in the production stage, models are often deployed into real-time scoring processes (scoring engines, web services, etc.).

2. Approval process
   a. Traditional: standard QA and approval processes.
   b. AnalyticOps: expansive and in-depth information review and reporting processes. These can include model training

and evaluation reports, champion versus challenger reports, and so forth, that are specific to individual models, frameworks, and/or use cases, providing more information as to project status and progress. It is essential to have adaptable, flexible approval processes.

3. Model management

   a. Traditional: number of applications or other components using the DevOps (development operations) approach is typically much smaller as DevOps typically handles complete applications or code packages.

   b. AnalyticOps: generates hundreds or even thousands of models that are deployed into production. Each of these models would need to have a full history of the model version: which framework was used, which data sets the model was trained with, information on model performance upon training, who deployed the model, where it was deployed, and so on.

A Guide to Embedding AnalyticOps

AnalyticOps, and embedding intelligence throughout the enterprise, requires a holistic approach to the project. It starts with determining the scope of your project. Understand what problems you have, and which of those are most cost-effective to solve with the pilot. These are within your initial scope. The project can scale by adding to the scope, but *not* before demonstrating success in solving those problems that lie within the initial scope. Do not—repeat—do not scale up before you demonstrate success, or you will become one of the 85% of pilot failures.

> At its core, AnalyticOps is outcomes driven. Success is measured by how well the initiative meets your goals.

It's also critical to precisely define the outcomes of your analytics initiative. It's been said that you can't build a road until you know where you're going. At its core, AnalyticOps is outcomes driven. Success is measured by how well the initiative meets your goals. This sounds self-evident, but it's amazing how often companies tend to focus on analytics tools, and their capabilities, rather than how those capabilities will actually help them achieve their analytics goals. Tools are not the objective—outcomes are.

Your outcomes should be targeted to the problems you have. They should be quantitatively measurable. They should inform your decision-making at every point in the process *and* shape the processes within which you embed your analytics capabilities. Tools should only be facilitators in achieving your desired outcomes. They are a means to an end.

Finally, it's crucial to involve stakeholders from across your organization to participate in, and champion, the project. Don't just bring them in for window dressing. Listen to them and value their opinions. They're on the frontlines and know what they need to do their jobs. Stakeholders play a large part in determining the success or failure of your project.

AnalyticOps in Action

Deploying AnalyticOps can produce quick, measurable results. Danske Bank, for example, is a 145-year-old Danish global bank with strong local roots and bridges to multinational financial markets, serving 2.7 million customers and 1,800 corporate institutions. Danske was losing tens of millions of Euros per month due to their inability to detect and prevent financial fraud from a variety of means—both customer initiated (fake invoice, beneficiary account changes) and fraudster initiated (spear phishing, identity theft).

Danske rapidly deployed an AnalyticOps framework with advanced, continuous deep learning and operationalizing capabilities that allowed them to achieve a 35% increase in fraud detection rate, a 25% reduction in false positives, automation of new models into production, and the ability to combat new fraud challenges as they were identified.

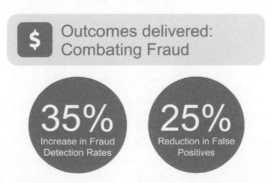

Figure 10.4

AnalyticOps to Enable Pervasive Intelligence

AnalyticOps is the foundation for pervasive data intelligence. It is the vehicle that will enable you to industrialize the intelligence capabilities you need for better decision-making and embed those capabilities into every facet of your organization.

The productionalization of analytics capabilities gives you the ability to see across organizational divisions and utilize analytics at scale. With AnalyticOps, you can quickly develop and deploy mission-critical applications to gain the insight and intelligence you need to solve your most complex business issues and drive those outcomes that will thrust you beyond competitiveness to dominance.

CHAPTER 11

Intelligent Clouds— Combining the Cloud and Analytics to Realize Pervasive Intelligence

According to a recent IDG survey, about 70% of companies have at least one application in the cloud. An additional 43% want to migrate most or all of their data workloads—and, significantly, their analytics capabilities—to the cloud over the next few years. To be sure, cloud adoption is growing due to pressures—both internal and external—to make data intelligence pervasive and increase agility and responsiveness to market changes, shrink data center footprints, adapt to changing intelligence needs, and move IT costs from CapEx to OpEx.

However, cloud adoption plans are often hindered by concerns about security and the lack of IT staff with experience to manage a cloud environment. As a result, many companies struggle to identify the cloud model that's right for their goals. One model that can help you meet your goals, regardless of your size or resource capabilities, is intelligent clouds as-a-service.

THE INTELLIGENT CLOUD

Intelligent clouds contain analytics and cloud storage, bundled as a managed-services package—typically on a subscription basis—that can be scaled up or down quickly, at will, depending on your needs. They allow you to deploy the latest and most sophisticated analytics capabilities you need, combined with flexible, secure cloud storage that fits your workload size and operational requirements.

THE BENEFITS OF INTELLIGENCE

With an intelligent cloud, your focus shifts from wrangling your IT infrastructure to leveraging sophisticated analytics capabilities and large data sets, so you can gain faster, deeper insights into your business to improve performance and outcomes. How?

> With an intelligent cloud, your focus shifts from wrangling your IT infrastructure to leveraging sophisticated analytics capabilities and large data sets, so you can gain faster, deeper insights into your business to improve performance and outcomes.

- You get predictability, both in performance and cost. You pay only for the storage and analytics capabilities you need, and you can scale up or down quickly, depending on your everyday workloads, or any special projects that you might wish to undertake. This gives you resource efficiency and more from your technology investments. It's an awesome capability to have when you're responding to ever-changing competitive and market conditions.

- You get peace of mind. You don't have to worry about your data or your analytics capabilities. If you have a DBA on staff, that person can manage the interaction between you and your cloud/analytics partner. Otherwise, the infrastructure management and the analytics capabilities are taken care of—not to mention the security of your data and applications. The entire process is managed for you, to enable you to focus on your business, not your IT infrastructure.

- You get availability. Because the process is managed for you, and it's infinitely, immediately scalable depending on your needs, your analytics and storage capabilities are there when you need them, as you need them. Most cloud/analytics vendors will guarantee performance in their SLAs. Can you do that by managing your own infrastructure? Probably not. Also, because your needs can change, and you need ultimate flexibility, most analytics/cloud vendors will offer options to go with public clouds like Amazon Web Services or Microsoft Azure, their own hosted clouds, or a hybrid thereof. It's the ultimate mix of scalability and flexibility.

  It's clear that intelligent clouds as-a-service can help you maximize your efficiency and focus on boosting your analytics outcomes, but there are some things you need to look out for when choosing a vendor partner to manage your intelligent cloud.

- Performance guarantees. Best-in-class vendor partners will guarantee 99.5%+availability. That lessens the possibility of downtime for mission-critical applications and gives you the confidence to undertake large-scale projects with big workloads, without worrying about whether you can scale up or have access to your data and apps when you need it.

■ Security. The best vendors will offer sophisticated security with excellent encryption and monitoring capabilities. They shouldn't ever see or touch your data in the process. The SLA should clearly spell out security measures and guarantees to give you peace of mind as your workload migrates from your control to theirs.

■ Superior customer service and management. Subscription and pricing models should be flexible and customizable to match your needs—now and in the future. Top vendors will offer some sort of easy-to-use portal system where your DBA can perform tasks such as scaling up or down, viewing metrics, starting and stopping the database, scheduling backups, and setting firewall and security parameters. Your SLA should also offer 24/7 customer service, or at least 24-hour service during the work week.

PERVASIVE INTELLIGENCE VIA THE INTELLIGENT CLOUD

There are almost infinite cloud service models out there, and it's crucial to your success in realizing pervasive intelligence and driving those high-impact outcomes to choose the right one for your business. Intelligent clouds, with their flexibility and performance, can be that right choice for any business, large or small.

Conclusion

What should be clear from reading this book is that analytics capabilities are necessary, but they are not a product in themselves. Analytics implementation is not the goal. Instead, the function of analytics is to help you make data intelligence pervasive in your organization so that you can define and achieve game-changing outcomes.

There is also no single path that all companies traverse to realize those high-impact outcomes. Although it's a cliché to say it, pervasive intelligence is a journey that you undertake with the goal of getting better insights into your business so that you can make better decisions and grow your bottom line.

That journey won't be finished—ever. There will always be new technologies and deployment frameworks, and there will always be new theories about how to use those technologies and frameworks effectively. What won't change, however, is the fact that if you leverage analytics effectively, that is, you let your business lead the way in defining which capabilities are needed to do the job, and you select the correct tools and technical infrastructure to deploy those capabilities, you have a good chance of making intelligence pervasive throughout your organization and of achieving those high-impact outcomes.

Achieving pervasive intelligence isn't easy—as nothing worthwhile ever is—but it is worth it. It's worth investing in defining your high-impact outcomes, in trying to understand the value of your information, in transformative technologies like intelligent clouds and artificial intelligence and machine learning, in effective security to protect your data and your customers, and in operationalizing analytics throughout your organization.

If you take nothing else away from this book, take the idea that it's never too late to correct mistakes you might have made along your journey to more effective, ubiquitous organizational intelligence. Believe that you can change, do the hard things that need to be done, get champions on board with your ideas, and set your plans in motion—using what you know and taking all the help you can get from trusted advisors. You can do this—so what are you waiting for?

Index

Page references in *italics* refer to figures.